THE OFFICIAL  SPORT

RUGBY WORLD CUP GUIDE 2007

First published by Carlton Books 2007

Copyright © Carlton Books Limited 2007

ITV Sport and ITV Sport logo used under licence from Granada Ventures Ltd.

Carlton Books Limited
20 Mortimer Street
London W1T 3JW

A CIP catalogue record for this book is available from the British Library

ISBN: 978-1-84442-875-5

Commissioning Editor: Martin Corteel
Project Art Editor: Darren Jordan
Editorial Assistant: David Ballheimer
Designer: Ben Ruocco
Picture Research: Paul Langan
Production: Peter Hinton

Printed in Dubai

PUBLISHER'S NOTES

All statistics correct to the end of the Six Nations Championship,
17 March 2007.

All kick-off times given are local time.

This book has been prepared without any involvement on the part of the
International Rugby Board or any related bodies. Carlton Books is not
affiliated or associated with the International Rugby Board in any way.

ABOUT THE AUTHOR

Chris Hawkes, a former youth international and first-class cricketer
with Leicestershire CCC (1990–92), is an experienced writer and editor,
specializing in sport, who has worked on numerous titles for an array of
publishers on an assortment of subjects. He lives in London.

France expects: Following home success in football's 1984 European Championships
and the 1998 World Cup, French fans will be hoping they won't be singing the Blues
come the 2007 Rugby World Cup. The nation awaits ...

THE OFFICIAL itv SPORT

RUGBY WORLD CUP GUIDE 2007

CHRIS HAWKES

CARLTON
BOOKS

Contents

INTRODUCTION

Rugby needed the World Cup. The very things that made the sport's governing body procrastinate for so long have unashamedly taken the sport to another level and it has become a tournament that is eagerly embraced by players and fans alike. No longer was it enough to be crowned the champions of European rugby or the Kings of the Tasman divide: the teams needed to know who were the world's number one and fans across the world deserved the chance to obtain bragging rights for a four-year period. It may be to the detriment of the Six Nations and Tri-Nations tournament, but every sport needs a world champion and, make no bones about it, the Rugby World Cup is the one trophy every team wants.

What's more, the tournament has become a staggering success, and not just on the field of play. Commercially, only the Olympic Games and the FIFA World Cup generate more income: more than four billion people around the globe are expected to tune into France 2007 – that cannot be anything but good news for the sport's profile – and more than one million spectators are expected to flock to France to enjoy the game's greatest spectacle.

But it is a tournament that still has its critics. The nay-sayers will point to the fact that the gulf between rugby's haves and have-nots is as wide as ever and that the tournament itself is still littered with too many meaningless games – 58 percent of the matches at the last World Cup had a points differential of over 20 (the highest since the inaugural tournament in 1987). Be that as it may, who could deny the likes of Georgia, Portugal and Namibia their moment of glory on the game's greatest stage. Just as is the case with other sports, simply taking part can give some countries the greatest cause for cheer.

And the tournament could not have chosen a better location. It is to the game's credit that the event will be staged in many of the venues that hosted the highly successful 1998 FIFA World Cup; it is a far cry from the inaugural tournament in 1987 when many of the matches were staged in obscure venues that amounted to little more than provincial club grounds. And what an opportunity it will present to the thousands upon thousands of fans: there can be few better places to be than France in the autumn.

Of course, every Frenchman and his cockerel will be hoping that his country can repeat the feat of the football team and lift the World Cup for the first time on home soil: New Zealand did it in 1987 and South Africa in 1995 and home advantage will see the French as strong tournament contenders. Meanwhile, the All Blacks, the powerhouse of world rugby, will be desperate to shake off their tag as World Cup underachievers and end their 20-year wait for more World Cup glory. Will England be able to do what no other team has been able to achieve and defend their crown? Or will Australia make it a hat-trick of World Cup wins, all in the northern hemisphere? Maybe Ireland, Wales or Scotland can shake off the memories of multiple World Cup disappointments? The entire rugby world cannot wait to find out.

The Arc de Triomphe: Commissioned in 1806 by Emperor Napoleon I to commemorate victory at Austerlitz and completed some 30 years later, the Arc has become one of the world's most famous landmarks and one of *the* symbols of France.

ABOUT THE WORLD CUP

WELL WORTH THE WAIT

One hundred and sixteen long years passed between the staging of the first ever rugby Test match – played between England and Scotland at Edinburgh in 1871 – and the first World Cup in 1987, and although the idea of holding a tournament along the lines of the FIFA World Cup had been voiced several times, it was rejected on each occasion. Rugby fans everywhere are glad the opposition finally waned.

The principal objection had been that a tournament of such status would have been run by commercial operators and, as such, would have challenged the amateur principle of the game. The nay-sayers, primarily members of the Home Union boards (England, Ireland, Scotland and Wales), feared that such a tournament would change the game irrevocably. They were spot on.

But Australia and New Zealand continued to promote the idea and in both 1983 and 1984 they put forward proposals to host the tournament. This prompted the IRB to instigate a World Cup feasibility study; Australia and New Zealand formed a working group and the results of their study were presented to the IRB in Paris on 20–21 March 1985. The outcome of that

hearing ensured rugby would never be the same again.

Voting on the concept is now a part of rugby folklore. Australia, France and New Zealand were for the idea; the Home Unions were fervently against. But South Africa still had to vote. In the full knowledge that they were facing a long period of isolation from world sport, they decided in favour; it squared the votes at 4–4. There was a stalemate. The discussions started all over again. England rescinded. They were soon followed by Wales and the die had been cast.

And although the first tournament could have been described more as a meeting of old friends – it was an invitation-only affair – it has grown up considerably during its five previous incarnations. Now firmly established as one of the world's premier sporting events, the 2007 World Cup in France will attract more than 700,000 spectators from English-speaking countries alone during September and October 2007 and the games will be screened to more than four billion television viewers via 250 separate television networks.

Bidding for the 2007 World Cup started back in 2001 and was a two-horse race from the outset. England and France – who had sat on opposite sides of the fence back in the 1980s and who had both been part of jointly hosted tournaments – applied to be sole hosts of rugby's sixth World Cup. In April 2002, it was announced that France had secured the IRB's vote by the staggering margin of 18–3.

France is no stranger to hosting major sporting events. It has hosted the Olympic Games twice (1900 and 1924), the Winter Olympics three times (1924, 1968 and 1992), the FIFA World Cup twice (1938 and 1998), the UEFA European Championships twice (1960 and 1984), the World Athletic Championships (in 2003) and the Tour de France annually since 1903. It is a country steeped in sporting tradition.

Rugby's Holy Grail: Just 38cm high, silver gilded in gold and supported by two cast scroll handles, the William Webb Ellis Cup is the most sought-after trophy in world rugby. Who will be the next team to get their hands on it?

Dancing in the streets: FIFA World Cup success in 1998 led to millions converging on the streets of Paris. Expect a repeat performance if Les Bleus can match the feat of their footballing compatriots.

KNOW THE GAME

POOL PHASE

The tournament's 20 nations have been drawn into four pools of five teams. Each team will play the other team in its pool on a round-robin basis. Four points will be awarded for a win, two for a draw and one for a defeat. After the completion of the ten pool matches, the top two teams will progress to the quarter-finals as the pool winner and the pool runners-up.

If two teams finish the pool stage level on points, the higher-ranked team will be determined in the following way:

(i) the winner of the match between the two tied teams will be ranked higher;

(ii) if still level, the team with the higher points difference between points scored and points conceded will be ranked higher;

(iii) if still level, the team with the best difference between tries scored and tries conceded will be ranked higher;

(iv) if still level, the team that has scored the higher number of points in the pool stages will be ranked higher;

(v) if still level, the side that has scored the greater number of tries in the pool matches will be ranked higher;

(vi) if still level, the team with the higher ranking in the Official IRB world rankings on 1 October 2007 will be ranked higher.

KNOCKOUT MATCHES
Quarter-finals

The top two teams from each group will progress to the last eight and the quarter-final line-ups will be determined in the following way:

QF1: Winner Pool B v. Runner-up Pool A
QF2: Winner Pool C v. Runner-up Pool D
QF3: Winner Pool A v. Runner-up Pool B
QF4: Winner Pool D v. Runner-up Pool C

If the teams are tied at full-time, the following will apply to determine the winner:

(i) following a break of five minutes, a period of extra-time will follow, consisting of two periods of ten minutes with a five-minute interval in between;

(ii) if the teams are still tied, they will enter a period of sudden death in which the first team to score a point will be deemed the winner;

(iii) if the period of sudden death has not resulted in a winner, the teams will take part in a kicking competition, the winner of which will be declared the winner of the match.

The winners of the quarter-finals will progress to the semi-finals.

Semi-finals

The semi-final line-ups will be determined in the following manner:
SF1: Winner QF1 v. Winner QF2
SF2: Winner QF3 v. Winner QF4

In the event of a match ending in a tie following normal time, the same criteria used for the quarter-finals will be used to determine the winner. The winners will progress to the final; the losers will progress to a third-place play-off match.

Third-place play-off

This match will be contested between the two losing semi-finalists. In the event of a match ending in a tie following normal time, the same criteria used for the quarter-finals and semi-finals will be used to determine the winner.

Final

This match will be contested between the two winning semi-finalists. In the event of a match ending in a tie following normal time, the same criteria used for the quarter-finals and semi-finals will be used to determine the winner.

And in recent times the French have enjoyed considerable success every time they have hosted one of these major championships. Michel Platini inspired them to UEFA European Championship success in 1984; Zinedine Zidane's exploits at the FIFA World Cup in 1998 led to millions dancing in the Champs Elysées. But if the French rugby team want to enjoy such celebrated status among their countrymen, they will have to do what no northern hemisphere country has ever managed to achieve before: to lift the William Webb Ellis trophy on home soil.

It will be a familiar journey for French sports fans. The tournament will use many of the stadiums used in 1998 and memories of that, coupled with France's proximity to the British Isles, have seen ticket sales go through the roof: more than 170,000 tickets were sold on the first day and had hit the million mark by September 2006 – more than a year before the tournament kicked off. Expectation for the 2007 World Cup is high and there is little doubt that the sixth incarnation of rugby's greatest event will be the best yet.

Just run with it: The bronze statue of William Webb Ellis, now sitting proudly outside Rugby School in the English Midlands, captures the apocryphal moment when the game of rugby was said to have begun.

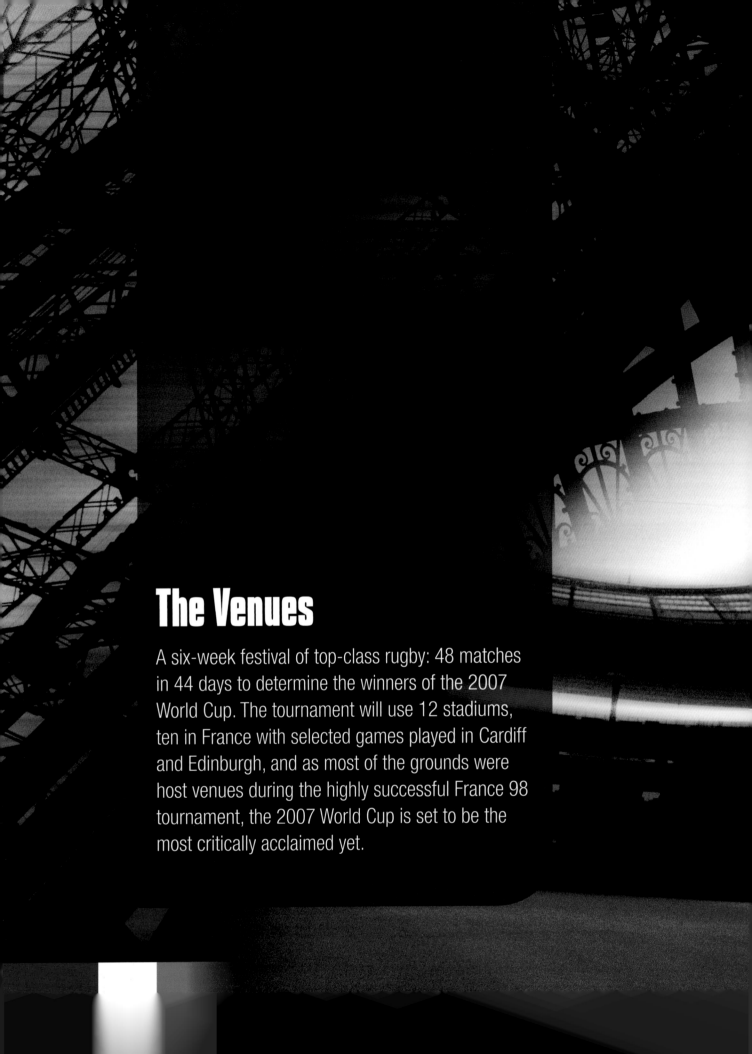

The Venues

A six-week festival of top-class rugby: 48 matches in 44 days to determine the winners of the 2007 World Cup. The tournament will use 12 stadiums, ten in France with selected games played in Cardiff and Edinburgh, and as most of the grounds were host venues during the highly successful France 98 tournament, the 2007 World Cup is set to be the most critically acclaimed yet.

THE VENUES

MAJOR TOURNAMENT PEDIGREE

None of the talk in the build-up to the sixth incarnation of the World Cup centred on the stadiums. Why? Because France's rich sporting pedigree is reflected in the numerous state-of-the-art stadiums dotted around the country. Throw the Millennium Stadium and Murrayfield into the already impressive mix and the stage for France 2007 is well and truly set.

STADE DE FRANCE, SAINT-DENIS
HOME TEAM: France *(football and rugby)*

The Stade de France will forever provoke fond memories for the French. It was there, on 12 July 1998, that Zinedine Zidane inspired his country to a 3–0 FIFA World Cup final win over Brazil to lift the Jules Rimet trophy for the first time. The Stade de France was the centrepiece of France's bid to stage the 1998 football World Cup and plans were finalized in 1992, after FIFA awarded France the competition. Construction on the site began in 1995 and, 31 months later, a state-of-the-art sporting facility housing an enormous roof was complete. The venue was also used to host athletics' 2003 World Championships.

Stade de France: The state-of-the-art stadium provided the stage for France's footballers to become world champions in 1998. Every French fan will be hoping for a repeat performance in 2007.

PARC DES PRINCES, PARIS
HOME TEAM: Paris-Saint-Germain *(football)*

From 1972 to 1997 the Parc des Princes was the home of France's national football and rugby teams. Built on land that formerly served as a woodland park for the French royal family, the first cycling track was built on the site in 1893. It was renovated in 1931 to cater for football and rugby teams and again in 1967 to facilitate to construction of Paris's ring road – the Périphérique. During its long history, the Parc des Princes has hosted two football World Cups (in 1938 and 1998), France's 1984 European Championship final success, the climax of every Tour de France staged between 1903 and 1967, and hosted matches in both the 1991 and 1999 Rugby World Cups.

Parc des Princes: It became an almost impregnable fortress during its 25 years as the home of French rugby.

LENS
STADE FÉLIX-BOLLAERT *41,500*

GROUP A

| ENGLAND v. USA | 8 SEPTEMBER |
| SOUTH AFRICA v. TONGA | 22 SEPTEMBER |

GROUP D

| GEORGIA v. NAMIBIA | 26 SEPTEMBER |

SAINT-DENIS, PARIS
STADE DE FRANCE *80,000*

GROUP A

| ENGLAND v. SOUTH AFRICA | 14 SEPTEMBER |

GROUP D

| FRANCE v. ARGENTINA | 7 SEPTEMBER |
| FRANCE v. IRELAND | 21 SEPTEMBER |

QUARTER-FINAL 4

| WINNER GROUP D v. RUNNER-UP GROUP C | 7 OCTOBER |

SEMI-FINAL 1

| WINNER QUARTER-FINAL 1 v. WINNER QUARTER-FINAL 2 | 13 OCTOBER |

SEMI-FINAL 2

| WINNER QUARTER-FINAL 3 v. WINNER QUARTER-FINAL 4 | 14 OCTOBER |

FINAL — 20 OCTOBER

LYON
STADE GERLAND *43,051*

GROUP B

| AUSTRALIA v. JAPAN | 8 SEPTEMBER |

GROUP C

| NEW ZEALAND v. PORTUGAL | 15 SEPTEMBER |

GROUP D

| ARGENTINA v. GEORGIA | 11 SEPTEMBER |

PARIS
PARC DES PRINCES *50,000*

GROUP A

| SOUTH AFRICA v. SAMOA | 9 SEPTEMBER |
| ENGLAND v. TONGA | 28 SEPTEMBER |

GROUP C

| ITALY v. PORTUGAL | 19 SEPTEMBER |

GROUP D

| IRELAND v. ARGENTINA | 30 SEPTEMBER |

THIRD-PLACE PLAY-OFF — 19 OCTOBER

NANTES
STADE LA BEAUJOIRE *38,285*

GROUP A

| ENGLAND v. SAMOA | 22 SEPTEMBER |

GROUP B

| WALES v. CANADA | 9 SEPTEMBER |
| WALES v. FIJI | 29 SEPTEMBER |

MARSEILLE
STADE VÉLODROME *60,000*

GROUP C

| NEW ZEALAND v. ITALY | 8 SEPTEMBER |
| ITALY v. ROMANIA | 12 SEPTEMBER |

GROUP D

| ARGENTINA v. NAMIBIA | 22 SEPTEMBER |
| FRANCE v. GEORGIA | 30 SEPTEMBER |

QUARTER-FINAL 1

| WINNER GROUP B v. RUNNER-UP GROUP A | 6 OCTOBER |

QUARTER-FINAL 3

| WINNER GROUP A v. RUNNER-UP GROUP B | 7 OCTOBER |

SAINT-ETIENNE
STADE GEOFFROY-GUICHARD *36,000*

GROUP A

| SAMOA v. USA | 26 SEPTEMBER |

GROUP C

| SCOTLAND v. PORTUGAL | 9 SEPTEMBER |
| SCOTLAND v. ITALY | 29 SEPTEMBER |

BORDEAUX
CHABAN-DELMAS STADIUM *35,200*

GROUP B

| CANADA v. JAPAN | 25 SEPTEMBER |
| AUSTRALIA v. CANADA | 29 SEPTEMBER |

GROUP D

| IRELAND v. NAMIBIA | 9 SEPTEMBER |
| IRELAND v. GEORGIA | 15 SEPTEMBER |

TOULOUSE
LE STADE *37,000*

GROUP B

| JAPAN v. FIJI | 12 SEPTEMBER |

GROUP C

| ROMANIA v. PORTUGAL | 25 SEPTEMBER |
| NEW ZEALAND v. ROMANIA | 29 SEPTEMBER |

GROUP D

| FRANCE v. NAMIBIA | 16 SEPTEMBER |

MONTPELLIER
STADE DE LA MOSSON *35,500*

GROUP A

USA v. TONGA	12 SEPTEMBER
SAMOA v. TONGA	16 SEPTEMBER
SOUTH AFRICA v. USA	30 SEPTEMBER

GROUP B

| AUSTRALIA v. FIJI | 23 SEPTEMBER |

CARDIFF
MILLENNIUM STADIUM

EDINBURGH
MURRAYFIELD

see page 15

CHABAN-DELMAS STADIUM, BORDEAUX

HOME TEAM: Bordeaux *(rugby)*, Bordeaux Girondins *(football)*

Opened to great fanfare for the 1938 football World Cup quarter-final match between Brazil and Czechoslovakia – a game Brazil won 2–1 – the Chaban-Delmas Stadium (above), previously known as Parc Lescure, but renamed after the city's mayor from 1947–95, is a classic example of 1930s neoclassical school architecture: its details, curves, décor and shapes reek of modernity. As such, it has earned a listing as one of France's favourite monuments. Renovated and enlarged for the 1998 FIFA World Cup, it is home to Bordeaux Girondins FC and Bordeaux rugby club, who won the French championship in 1969 and 1991.

STADE VÉLODROME, MARSEILLE

HOME TEAM: Olympique de Marseille *(football)*

Simply the home of "OM", the much-storied French football team that is as much of a religion in these parts as croissants and strong coffee in the morning. But in recent times the Stade Vélodrome has become quite a fortress for the French rugby team, too – some people would go as far as to say that the French are nigh on unbeatable there. Inaugurated for the 1938 FIFA World Cup it has since undergone numerous renovations, most recently for the 1998 edition. A rather quaint touch is that each of the four stands is named after a local celebrity, such as Chevalier Roze, a citizen who brought an end to the plague in the city in 1720.

STADE FÉLIX-BOLLAERT, LENS

HOME TEAM: Lens *(football)*

The very fact the Stade Félix-Bollaert was named as a venue for the 2007 World Cup came as a surprise. Other than in Paris, little or no rugby is played north of the River Loire and Lens is the beneficiary of the French rugby board's desire to spread the rugby gospel. Stade Félix-Bollaert is a football stadium. Completed in 1932, it was modernized when France hosted the football European Championships in 1984 and again for the 1998 FIFA World Cup. But it has played host to major international rugby matches too: most notably when Argentina beat Ireland 28–24 in a World Cup quarter-final play-off match in 1999.

STADE DE LA MOSSON, MONTPELLIER

HOME TEAM: Montpellier-Hérault SC *(football)*

Set in the north-eastern part of Montpellier, a young university city in the south of France that is home to the oldest medical faculty in Europe, the Stade de la Mosson (below) is named after the river that flows next to it; it paid the price for its location in 2002 when it suffered flood damage. Home to the Montpellier-Hérault football team, the stadium has also played host to some important rugby matches, such as the semi-final of the French championship between Stade Toulousain and Bourgoin in 1999. It was also used as a venue for France 98.

STADE GERLAND, LYON

HOME TEAM: Olympique Lyonnais *(football)*

The Rugby World Cup's foray into the world of football continues with the Stade Gerland (below), the home of Olympique Lyonnais, the side that has dominated French domestic football in recent times. The stadium's original design was inspired by an amphitheatre and was opened in 1926 as a cycle track (it hosted several stages of the Tour de France). It was demolished in the 1960s and rebuilt as a football stadium, going on to host matches in the 1984 European Championships and France 98. It was for the latter that the stadium was turned into a modern state-of-the-art sports facility.

STADE LA BEAUJOIRE, NANTES

HOME TEAM: FC Nantes-Atlantique *(football)*

When French football supporters think of Nantes, they are transported back to 16 June 1984 and France's European Championship match against Belgium. Michel Platini scored a hat-trick, France romped to a 5–0 win and victory over their neighbours was sweet. That day, 51,000 spectators cheered on their heroes, a figure dramatically reduced by the time renovations had been completed for France 98. The Stade la Beaujoire has also been a successful venue for the French rugby team; they have notched up five wins there, including their 24–3 win over New Zealand in 1990.

STADE GEOFFROY-GUICHARD, SAINT-ETIENNE
HOME TEAM: Saint-Etienne *(football)*

The Stade Geoffroy-Guichard is home to the club team that thrilled France in 1976 when it made it all the way to the European Cup final at Hampden Park, Glasgow, only to lose 1–0 to Bayern Munich. Saint-Etienne, who wear green and white in honour of the club's owners – a distribution company called Casino – have since gone on to compile one of the most impressive records in French football, with ten championship titles and six French Cup wins to their name. The stadium was used as a venue for football's 1984 European Championships and again for the 1998 World Cup.

LE STADE, TOULOUSE
HOME TEAM: Toulouse *(football)*

To travel to Toulouse is to step into the epicentre of French rugby and the Sept-Deniers stadium, home of French powerhouse Stade Toulousain, is its beating heart. But another stadium in this southwest city has been chosen as a venue for the 2007 World Cup: Le Stade, home of the Toulouse football team and boasting 37,000 seats, which was first built in 1949. Renovated entirely in time for the 1998 FIFA World Cup, it received major structural damage in the AZF industrial disaster of 2001. It has since been refurbished and is more than ready to welcome world rugby's showpiece event through its doors.

MURRAYFIELD, EDINBURGH
CAPACITY: 67,500
HOME TEAM: Scotland *(rugby)*
MATCHES STAGED: Group C: Scotland v. Romania (18/09/2007); Scotland v. New Zealand (23/09/2007)

Built in 1925, Murrayfield has undergone major renovations over the years and, in 1994, its capacity was cut to 67,500 to comply with modern safety regulations. It has long been a fortress for Scottish rugby: many teams have visited seeking the last leg of a grand slam – most notably France (in 1984, 1986 and 1988) and England (1990 and 2000) – but, against the backdrop of the Tartan Army's haunting "Flower of Scotland" have left empty-handed and disappointed. And although the Scotland rugby team may have struggled on the road in recent times, Murrayfield has retained its reputation as a fortress.

MILLENNIUM STADIUM, CARDIFF
CAPACITY: 72,500
HOME TEAM: Wales *(football and rugby)*
MATCHES STAGED: Group B: Wales v. Australia (15/09/2007); Fiji v. Canada (16/09/2007); Wales v. Japan (20/09/2007)
Quarter-final 2: Winner Group C v. Runner-up Group D (06/10/2007)

Sitting proudly on the land that was once occupied by Cardiff Arms Park, the Millennium Stadium has risen from the dust of Welsh rugby's fortress and can be hailed as one of the great stadiums in world sport. Renovation work on the old Cardiff Arms Park began in 1997 in preparation for the 1999 World Cup, where it would host the opening and closing ceremonies, as well as the World Cup final. The result was a state-of-the-art stadium with a retractable roof and a playing surface that can be switched at 24 hours' notice. It is the home of both the Welsh football and rugby teams.

THE ROAD TO FRANCE

With the eight sides that made it through to the last eight of the 2003 World Cup gaining automatic entry for France 2007, 86 countries were left to fight it out for the remaining 12 World Cup berths. With almost 200 matches played on six continents it took more than two-and-a-half years, before the remaining 12 spots had been decided.

Africa (Qualifier: Namibia)

Qualification in the African section involved four rounds of matches with the winners of each phase qualifying automatically for the next phase, but it wasn't until round 2 that we finally arrived at the business end of proceedings. Here the teams were split into two pools: Pool 1, with Namibia, Kenya and Tunisia; and Pool 2, with Morocco, Ivory Coast and Uganda. The winners of each pool would then play each other on a home-and-away basis with the aggregate points winner over the two games gaining automatic entry to the World Cup.

Namibia, who had qualified via this process for the last two World Cups, opened their account with an 82–12 victory over Kenya in Windhoek. It would prove a significant result. Tunisia shocked Namibia (24–7), Kenya shocked first Tunisia (25–21) and then perhaps themselves when they beat Namibia 30–26 in Nairobi to leave the southern Africans' World Cup qualification chances hanging by a thread. But the Kenyans' 31–12 reverse against Tunisia two weeks later gave Namibia renewed hope: courtesy of their huge opening win, any form of victory over Tunisia in the final game would guarantee their pool victory on points difference. They won 23–15.

It was altogether more straightforward in pool B. Morocco seized the early initiative with an opening 36–3 win over Uganda and they never let it go. Their 9–9 away draw with Ivory Coast coupled with the Ivorians surprise 32–7 reverse against Uganda, virtually assured their safe passage to the next phase and they guaranteed

their place in the play-off showdown with Namibia with two final victories. But it was the southern Africans who won the prize. An aggregate 52–15 win for Namibia completed their qualification hat-trick, but all was not lost for Morocco: in the future lay a play-off against Portugal.

Americas (Qualifiers: Argentina, Canada, USA)

Although labelled under the Americas umbrella this was very much two separate tournaments that would only be rolled into one at the latter stages. The "champions" of North America and South America would take the first two automatic qualification spots and the two "runners-up" would face off to determine the third, with the loser of that game facing a repechage match with the winner of the Africa–Europe play-off.

There could have been no firmer favourite than Argentina to win the southern section. By the time the Pumas entered the qualification fray, Brazil had already passed through round 1b – notching up an impressive 73–3 win over Peru in São Paulo. Then Chile grabbed the headlines, seeing off Paraguay and Brazil to secure their place in the three-team round robin along with Argentina and Uruguay.

They may have wished they hadn't bothered. The Pumas were in no mood for upsets and duly ran out comfortable 60–13 winners in Santiago. A routine 26–0 home win over Uruguay followed to confirm Argentina's safe passage to France, and Uruguay's final-game 43–15 win over Chile ensured the runners-up spot and meant their World Cup qualification hopes were still very much alive.

It was a similar story in the northern section. Barbados battled their way through to the final qualification round only to be put to the sword by both the United States and Canada. It meant the North American neighbours would face off for an automatic qualification spot. Canada produced one of the performances of the entire campaign with a crushing 56–7 victory, but any

disappointment the Americans may have suffered was quickly put to one side when they notched up a comfortable 75–20 aggregate victory over Uruguay to book their passae to France. Uruguay, on the other hand, faced a nervous wait for the repechage matches.

Asia (Qualifier: Japan)

The process to determine the one Asian automatic qualification place may have been the epitome of perfect logic – coupled with an underlying sense of giving everybody a fair crack of the whip – but when Japan (the undisputed kings of Asian rugby), Korea and Hong Kong kick-started the process in May 2005, nobody would have bet against the same three teams meeting again a year and a half later in the three-team round robin final qualifiers.

Japan opened their qualification account with a statement of intent, crushing a hapless Hong Kong 91–3 in Tokyo, and followed up with a comfortable 50–31 away win over Korea, who subsequently confirmed their reputation as the region's second-best team with a 56–3 win over Hong Kong, who had been demoted to division two.

In round 2, the Arabian Gulf effectively stepped into Hong Kong's shoes in division one … and fared no better – they lost out 82–9 to Japan and 20–5 to Korea. Meanwhile, back in division two, Hong Kong, with wins over Sri Lanka (45–14) and China (23–7) duly confirmed their promotion back up to division one.

So when we finally arrived at the business end of the convoluted qualification process in November 2006, it was very much a case of as you were. The three sides who had started it renewed acquaintance in Hong Kong to determine who would gain the region's automatic qualification spot. Japan outclassed Hong Kong in the opening game. Korea did the same three days later, and then Japan confirmed their status as Asia's No.1 by brushing aside Korea 54–0. The

Cherry Blossoms were on their way to France. Korea, on the other hand, were off to Auckland for a repechage encounter with Tonga.

Europe (Qualifiers: Italy, Romania, Georgia)

Starting way back in September 2004, the European region saw by far the most extensive qualification process. Some 79 games had taken place – involving the likes of Andorra (who opened their campaign with an impressive 76–3 win over Norway), Finland and Slovenia – and 25 months had passed before the true qualification nitty-gritty started in earnest in October 2006 when the big boys of European rugby's second division finally entered the fray.

The fifth round saw Italy, Portugal and Russia matched up in Pool A and Georgia, Romania and Spain in Pool B. The winners of each pool would gain automatic World Cup qualification, with the runners-up meeting in a play-off to determine the third automatic qualification spot. The loser of that match then faced the daunting prospect of entering the repechage lottery – they would face the second-placed African team in a play-off to earn the right to face the fourth-placed Americas team.

Italy showed just how far they have come in recent times when they crushed Portugal 83–0 in L'Aquila in their opening game, and their subsequent 67–7 win over Russia in Moscow saw them ease to what will be their sixth consecutive World Cup appearance. Meanwhile, Portugal's tense 26–23 home win over Russia meant that their dreams of ensuring World Cup qualification for the first time were kept very much alive.

Romania were the class outfit in Pool B, beating both Georgia (20–8) and Spain (43–20) to ensure their place at France 2007, while Georgia's 37–23 win over Spain took them into the play-off with Portugal. A 17–3 Georgian win in Tblisi followed by an 11–11 draw in Lisbon saw Georgia secure a second consecutive World Cup appearance. Portugal? They would have to train for an extra series of repechage matches.

Oceania (Qualifiers: Samoa, Fiji)

The two automatic qualification places on offer would be determined in the following way. The lesser nations would fight it out for the right to face the lowest-placed team of the Fiji-Samoa-Tonga round robin in a play-off match up for a spot in the repechage matches.

Papua New Guinea and the Cook Islands were the class acts of round 1a, before the Cook Islands

won the two-legged play-off – they won 37–12 at home and lost 20–11 away – on points difference to progress to the next phase.

The focus of attention now shifted to the Fiji, Samoa and Tonga games. Make no mistake about it, these are important matches. All three teams were firmly expecting to qualify and these results would determine which World Cup groups the teams would go into. When it comes to World Cup qualification matches, these are the games you want to see.

Things didn't get any better for Tonga following their opening 19–11 defeat to Fiji. They ended up losing all four games, most of them convincingly, to leave Samoa and Fiji to fight it out for the region's top honours. Samoa finally took the laurels on points difference. But it wasn't all over for Tonga. They took all their recent frustrations out on the Cook Islands, crushing them 77–10 away and 90–0 at home to take their place in a one-off repechage showdown against Korea for a World Cup place.

Opposite: Kings of Africa: Namibia, led by Kees Lensing, were the class act of the African qualifying section.

Above: Power broker: Like the rest of Japan's side, Takuro Miuchi was too powerful for the opposition in the Asian qualifying section.

Below: Doing it the hard way: Epi Taione and his Tonga team were forced to go through the repechage round to qualify for the island's fifth World Cup appearance.

Repechage Round

This was the Last Chance Saloon as far as World Cup qualification was concerned. The first of the match-ups saw Tonga, still smarting from suffering the humiliation of having to secure their qualification via this route, face Korea, the team long considered the best Asian nation never to have made it to the World Cup. Tonga ensured Korea's long wait would continue with a crushing 85–3 win in Auckland.

In the second series of matches, Portugal battled past Morocco over two legs (10–5 in Casablanca and 16–15 in Lisbon), to face Uruguay in the fight for the last World Cup spot. Portugal won the first leg 12–5 in Lisbon and despite losing 18–12 in Montevideo, they qualified for the finals on points difference.

Qualifiers: Tonga, Portugal

REPECHAGE 1

| 20/01/2007 | Morocco | 5–10 | Portugal | Casablanca |
| 27/01/2007 | Portugal | 16–15 | Morocco | Lisbon |

Portugal wins play-off and will face Uruguay

| 10/03/2007 | Portugal | 12–5 | Uruguay | Lisbon |
| 24/03/2007 | Uruguay | 18–12 | Portugal | Montevideo |

Portugal qualify for the 2007 World Cup on points difference

REPECHAGE 2

| 10/02/2007 | Tonga | 85–3 | Korea | Auckland |

Tonga qualify for the 2007 World Cup

2007 WORLD CUP QUALIFIERS

AFRICA: Namibia **NORTH AMERICA:** Canada, USA
SOUTH AMERICA: Argentina **ASIA:** Japan
EUROPE: Italy, Romania, Georgia, Portugal **OCEANIA:** Samoa, Fiji, Tonga

The Teams

Twenty teams will battle it out for the right to be called world champions. New Zealand are the pre-tournament favourites; but they have been in that position before and have lifted the trophy only once. Defending champions England will be looking to become the first team to repeat as World Cup winners, whereas Australia will take some comfort from the fact that they have won the competition every time it has been staged in the northern hemisphere. France will also be looking for a World Cup first: no northern hemisphere country has ever lifted the trophy on home soil. For South Africa, a repeat of the form they showed in 1995 would give great cause for celebration. These are the major World Cup contenders: Ireland and Argentina have shown great form in the last two years, but are no more than strong outsiders; Wales, Scotland and Italy would be happy to make it through to the last eight; and, for the others, simply being there remains a great achievement.

PLAYING STRIP

White shirts with red trim, white shorts, black socks

FORM SINCE 2003 RUGBY WORLD CUP

Played:	38
Won:	16
Lost:	22
Drawn:	0
Winning percentage:	42.1%
Points for:	938
Points against:	875
Biggest victory:	70–0 v. Canada, 13 November 2004 at Twickenham
Heaviest defeat:	51–15 v. Australia, 26 June 2004 at Brisbane
Points scored per match:	24.7
Points conceded per match:	23.0

PAST WORLD CUP PERFORMANCES

1987	Quarter-finals
1991	Runners-up
1995	Semi-finals
1999	Quarter-finals
2003	CHAMPIONS

Phil Vickery: After suffering a string of injuries, the World Cup-winning prop made his return to England colours in the autumn internationals of 2006. Brian Ashton's first act in charge was to name the man they call "Raging Bull" as his captain.

ENGLAND

CHAMPIONS ON THE ROCKS

Jonny Wilkinson's World Cup-winning drop-goal seems a distant memory for most England fans. Seven straight defeats in 2006 prompted both a change of coach and captain and saw the 2003 winners slip to seventh in the world rankings. England's rugby stock had fallen to an all-time low.

On the face of it, the world champions' fall from grace came as no great surprise. By the time the team dubbed "Dad's Army" by the Australian press had lifted the game's ultimate prize on 22 November 2003 a number of influential players – including captain Martin Johnson – decided to bow out at the very top. The battle-hardened unit was starting to split up and, after a fall-out with the RFU, coach Clive Woodward soon followed. If that wasn't bad enough, their young points machine, Jonny Wilkinson, suffered a spate of injuries that kept him out of an England shirt for more than three years.

And how England missed them all. The world champions fell to Ireland (16–9 at Twickenham) and France (24–21 in Paris) in a disappointing 2004 Six Nations campaign. Then, following three comprehensive defeats at the hands of New Zealand (twice) and Australia on their summer tour to the southern hemisphere, England slumped to three defeats and finished fourth in the 2005 Six Nations points table; it was their worst showing since 1987.

And when a British Lions side packed with England players found themselves on the back end of an All Black whitewash in the summer of 2005, the country's rugby stock continued to fall. A 26–16 victory against Australia in the first of two autumn internationals did much to restore morale. A week later, they put up a spirited performance against New Zealand in a narrow 23–19 defeat, and when they followed that up with comfortable Six Nations wins over Wales (47–13) and Italy (31–16), it seemed as though England had rediscovered their old sense of swagger.

It was a false dawn. Scotland kicked their way to an 18–12 victory at Murrayfield. That was followed by England's worst performance for years, when they were flattened 31–6 in Paris and, with little left to play for but pride,

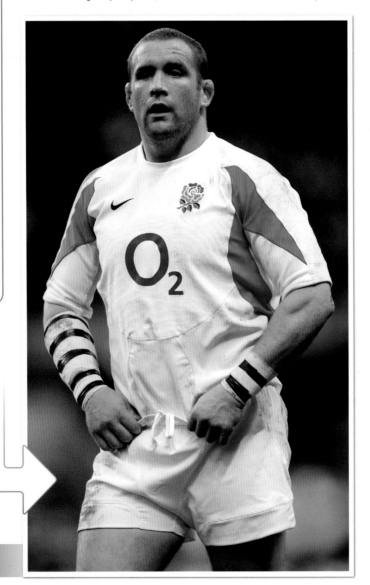

they slipped to a 28–24 defeat in Dublin to end another sorry campaign.

The southern hemisphere is no place for a team to find its form and an under-strength England lost both Tests against Australia, 34–3 in Sydney and 43–18 in Melbourne. But with senior players rested for the summer tour down under, greater things were expected of England in their 2006 autumn series of matches.

Instead, their losing run stretched to seven matches as first New Zealand (41–20) and then Argentina (25–18) grabbed the spoils at Twickenham. A 23–18 victory over South Africa a week later may have stopped the rot, but when the Springboks won seven days later something had to change. The axe finally fell on Andy Robinson's reign as coach, and Brian Ashton was charged with restoring England's rugby fortunes.

And following their performances in the 2007 Six Nations, which saw Jonny Wilkinson finally return from his injury nightmare and the introduction of a handful of new players, it seems as though the former Bath coach has done just that. England will look to defend their World Cup crown with some confidence. And so they should: it is a tournament in which they have some pedigree.

Not that they got off to the greatest of starts. In 1987, they never recovered from an opening 19–6 defeat against Australia and limped out of the tournament at the quarter-final stage following 16–3 defeat to Wales.

But it was an entirely different England team that marched to the final four years later. Following an opening defeat to New Zealand, England were ignited by a bruising 19–10 victory over France in Paris to set up a semi-final showdown against Scotland at Murrayfield. And, with a tense encounter deadlocked at 6–6 going into the final minutes, Rob Andrew squeezed a drop-goal between the posts to send England through to the World Cup final against Australia at Twickenham.

Perhaps spurred on by the pre-match observations of Australia's David Campese that England were a one-dimensional forward-oriented unit, England played an unusually expansive game in the final. But after taking the lead through a Tony Daly try, the Australian defence held firm and Campese had the last laugh.

England gained revenge four years later when Rob Andrew again knocked over the decisive drop-goal in England's 25–22 quarter-final victory over Australia. But then they ran into Jonah Lomu in rampaging mood and crashed to a 45–29 semi-final defeat.

And their showing in 1999 did little to clear the gathering gloom. Following a string of unconvincing performances in the group stages – including a 30–16 defeat to New Zealand – South Africa dumped them out of the tournament at the quarter-final stage. But then came 2003. The whole of England will be hoping for a dose of the same medicine.

 STAR PLAYER: Jonny Wilkinson

Position: Fly-half
Born: 25 May 1979, Frimley
Club: Newcastle Falcons
Height: 178cm **Weight:** 86kg
Debut: v. Ireland, 4 April 1998 at Twickenham
Caps: 55 **Points:** 919 (7t, 123c, 161p, 21dg)

A true star of the world game, Jonny Wilkinson is renowned for his obsessive approach to training and such dedication to his sport has seen him become one of the most feared outside-halves in world rugby. His precise boot and ability to control a match was a major contributory factor in England's 2003 World Cup success – his drop-goal in the dying seconds of extra-time in the Final clinched the match – and the succession of injuries that kept him out of an England shirt for more than three years thereafter undoubtedly contributed to England's slide down world rugby's pecking order. Everyone connected with the sport welcomed his return to the international fold in February 2007, and come the World Cup, he will be edging closer to the record for the most international points.

PLAYING STRIP

Green shirts with gold collars, white shorts, green socks

FORM SINCE 2003 RUGBY WORLD CUP

Played:	37
Won:	23
Lost:	13
Drawn:	1
Winning percentage:	62.2%
Points for:	1,082
Points against:	832
Biggest victory:	134–3 v. Uruguay, 11 June 2005 at East London
Heaviest defeat:	49–0 v. Australia, 15 July 2006 at Brisbane
Points scored per match:	29.2
Points conceded per match:	22.5

PAST WORLD CUP PERFORMANCES

1987	Did not enter
1991	Did not enter
1995	CHAMPIONS
1999	Semi-finals
2003	Quarter-finals

Percy Montgomery: The Namibian-born player is South Africa's leading points-scorer. He played a pivotal role in South Africa's 2004 Tri Nations Cup success, finishing the tournament as the leading points-scorer.

SOUTH AFRICA

REMEMBERING THE GOOD TIMES

When Nelson Mandela, wearing a replica No. 6 Springbok shirt, handed the World Cup to François Pienaar at Ellis Park following South Africa's dramatic final victory over New Zealand in 1995, a nation, one that had become united through rugby, danced in the streets. South Africa, as a country, had come a long, long way.

The International Rugby Board readmitted South Africa to the rugby fold in 1992 – after a nine-year stint in the wilderness – and one of its first acts thereafter was to award the country the 1995 World Cup. On the back of the first democratic elections in 1994, a new mood had overtaken South Africa and, as the start of the tournament approached, calls of "One Team One Nation" echoed around the country as the Proteas, as they were now to be called (the springbok was seen as a symbol of the Afrikaner era), experienced a remarkable surge in support – from the townships to the swanky suburbs of Johannesburg.

And following an emotional victory over defending champions Australia in Cape Town (27–18), the support continued to grow round by round. It reached a clamour as South Africa, the tournament's ninth seeds, brushed aside first Samoa in the quarter-finals (42–14) and then France in the semi-finals (19–15) to march all the way to a final showdown against New Zealand in Johannesburg. Roared on by a nation, the hosts stopped the All Blacks – and Jonah Lomu in particular – in their tracks, and Joel Stransky's extra-time drop-goal sealed a memorable win. The image of Pienaar hoisting the World Cup aloft, with an ecstatic Mandela by his side, will live for ever in the minds of many rugby fans.

But then things started to go wrong. Kitch Christie, the coach who had guided South Africa to the world crown, was forced to retire through illness – he died three years later. His replacement, André Markgraaf, came and went within a year. In 1997, a 2–1 series defeat to the British Lions and a record loss against New Zealand (55–35) saw the end of Carel Du Plessis's reign and it wasn't until Nick Mallett took charge that South Africa's rugby fortunes took a turn for the better.

Under Mallett, they recorded record victories over England (29–11) and Scotland (68–10). They then went on a 17-match unbeaten run, equalling the record of the

legendary 1965 All Blacks and taking the 1998 Tri Nations trophy in the process. The good times had returned. But the team had peaked too soon and when the 1999 World Cup came around, South Africa were terribly out of form.

Relying on a kicking game allied to their traditional forward strength, South Africa marched through the group stages and brushed aside the attentions of England in Paris in the quarter-finals, with Jannie De Beer kicking a World Cup record five drop-goals in a 44–21 victory. But that's where their journey came to an end, as South Africa lost out to Australia in a tense semi-final at Twickenham, 27–21. They had relinquished their grip on the world crown.

They never looked like getting it back four years later. A group match defeat to England (25–6) condemned them to a quarter-final against New Zealand. The All Blacks were too good for them and they crashed out of the competition following a 29–9 defeat. But the real turmoil came after the tournament, when details of the squad's pre-World Cup training trip to a military camp – Kamp Staaldraad (literally "Camp Steel Wire") – started to emerge.

In an attempt to increase team bonding, it was revealed that, among other things, players had been forced to climb naked into a foxhole and sing the national anthem while ice-cold water was being poured on them and versions of the English national anthem and the All Blacks' Haka were played to them at full volume. Amid public outcry, coach Rudolph Straeuli tended his resignation. Jake White took charge.

He got off to a dream start when, after losing their first two games, South Africa won their final two matches to end up winners of the most closely fought Tri Nations series ever played. The Boks were back: they swept the board at the end-of-season IRB awards, picking up the Best Team, Best Coach and Best Player awards (deserved recognition for some dynamic displays by their shock-haired flanker Schalk Burger).

They warmed up for the following year's Tri Nations with a record-breaking 134–3 win over Uruguay but, after losing their final match against New Zealand in Dunedin, 31–27, they finished runners-up. The critics started to voice their complaints. White had stayed faithful to the 2004 Tri Nations veterans at the expense of new talent and, according to the dissenting voices, this South Africa team was in decline.

Injuries forced White's hand. Burger suffered a serious neck injury against Scotland in June 2006 that kept him out of action for more than six months. By the time the 2006 Tri Nations came around, South Africa had several new players in the squad. They lost their opening game to Australia, 49–0, and only victories in their final two games saved them from humiliation, and an indifferent tour of Ireland and England later in the year did little to lift the mood.

Selection issues still abound, but if White gets the balance of his South Africa team right, they will be a handful for anyone.

COACH
Jake White
Having led the South Africa Under-21 side to World Cup victory in 2002, his appointment as national coach in 2004 seemed natural, but Jake White had inherited a team in turmoil. Renowned for his technical prowess, he led them to their first Tri Nations title since 1998. But things have not gone so well since, and a poor World Cup could well signal the end of his reign.

STAR PLAYER: John Smit

Position: Hooker/captain
Born: 3 April 1978, Pietersburg, South Africa
Club: Natal Sharks
Height: 188cm *Weight:* 116kg
Caps: 64 *Points:* 10 (2t)
Debut: v. Canada, 10 June 2000, East London

Tough, uncompromising and often on the receiving end of harsh words from the game's disciplinary committees, John Smit, a former South Africa Under-21 captain who used to ply his trade as a loosehead prop, has proved an inspired choice as captain. After making his debut against Canada as a 22-year-old in 2000, he was on and off the replacements' bench before a serious shoulder injury kept him out of the game for two years. He returned to South African colours for the 2003 World Cup and then, with the appointment of Jake White as coach, came his shock appointment as he became the 51st player to lead the South Africa side. He answered his critics in style, leading the Boks to the 2004 Tri Nations title and South Africa have won 22 out of his 35 Tests as captain.

PLAYING STRIP
Blue shirts with white trim, white shorts, white socks

FORM SINCE 2003 RUGBY WORLD CUP

Played:	14
Won:	7
Lost:	7
Drawn:	0
Winning percentage:	50.0%
Points for:	319
Points against:	335
Biggest victory:	53–9 v. Japan, 17 June 2006 at New Plymouth
Heaviest defeat:	74–7 v. Australia, 11 June 2005 at Sydney
Points scored per match:	22.8
Points conceded per match:	23.9

PAST WORLD CUP PERFORMANCES

1987	Did not enter
1991	Quarter-finals
1995	Quarter-finals
1999	Quarter-final play-offs
2003	Group stages

SAMOA

RUGBY'S BREEDING GROUND

A star-studded line-up, a third of whose players were of Samoan descent, crushed all before them during a Grand Slam-winning tour of the Home Nations in 2005. The problem was, as far as die-hard Samoan rugby fans were concerned, they were all wearing an All Blacks shirt.

Given the close association between the two countries – New Zealand administered Western Samoa between 1919 and 1962 and most Samoans are granted dual nationality – this eventuality shouldn't have come as much of a surprise. But it has led to great debates in world rugby, with Samoa often seen as little more than a development site for the next generation of All Blacks.

Samoa is hardly the innocent victim in all of this. It was Samoa's rugby authorities who instigated a recruitment policy to scour New Zealand's Samoan communities for the next "big thing" – many of whom had been born in New Zealand and who grew up dreaming of playing for the All Blacks – and who offered them the chance to play international rugby before they had even appeared on the radar of the New Zealand provincial selectors.

The problem came when they started to excel: the New Zealand selectors came knocking on their door, and the majority of the players concerned jumped at the chance to play for the country of their birth. The IRB finally intervened in 1994, stating that any player who had played for Samoa would have to undertake a three-year period of qualification before they could play for another country.

It wasn't perhaps the future the Marist brothers who brought the game to the islands 87 years ago would have predicted. Regular internationals weren't staged there until 1982, when Western Samoa – as they were called until 1995 – played in a Tri Nations series with Fiji and Tonga. They won. As such, there would have been widespread dismay when, in 1987, they were not among the nine invitees to play in the inaugural World Cup, particularly when Fiji and Tonga were among the chosen few.

And it was with just more than a sense of irony that Bryan Williams – the first Samoan-

Semo Sititi: Now plying his trade with the Borders team in Scotland, the Samoan captain is already a veteran of two World Cups.

born player to have transferred his allegiance to New Zealand – returned to the land of his birth in a coaching capacity to guide the islanders – containing Pat Lam, a New Zealand-born forward with Samoan ancestry – through a World Cup elimination series in Japan to secure their berth in the 1991 finals.

And what an impact they made. Ferocious defence and attacking flair saw them pull off a dramatic 16–13 victory over Wales in their opening fixture. A comfortable 35–12 win over Argentina followed before they lost out to eventual champions Australia (9–3) in their final group game. But they had done enough to earn a tough trip to face Scotland at Murrayfield in the quarter-finals. They ran out of steam, losing 28–6, but left the tournament as an established force in rugby's world elite.

Another fine showing in the 1995 World Cup in South Africa saw them reach the quarter-finals for the second tournament in a row, notching up wins over Italy (42–18) and Argentina (32–26) in the process. But they couldn't get past South Africa in the quarter-finals, losing 42–14.

The advent of professionalism in 1995 saw the islands needing to keep pace with the ever-changing rugby environment. The lure of professional contracts in New Zealand grew ever more tempting for up-and-coming Samoan players and the national board realized that they would be hard pushed to keep their momentum going and maintain their status as one of rugby's big boys.

Samoa put in more fine performances in the 1999 World Cup, opening up with a convincing 43–9 win against Japan before suffering a disappointing 32–16 loss to Argentina. To stay in the tournament Samoa had to emulate the Class of '91 and beat Wales, which they did, running out 38–31 winners. It set up a quarter-final play-off match against Scotland, but they lost 35–20.

The price for finishing second in their qualification group for the 2003 World Cup, on points difference to Fiji, was a place in a tough group containing England and South Africa. They lost out to both, despite having led England for most of the match, and failed to pass the first hurdle for the first time in their World Cup history.

By now, though, Samoan rugby had become a brand: its players were renowned for their ferocious tackling, their physical presence on the pitch and their sheer will to win and most English Premiership clubs had at least one of them on their books. But Samoa's success has worked against them. As most of their players ply their trade abroad, it has become increasingly difficult to get them together for training sessions. As a result, Samoa have played just 15 internationals since their exit from the last World Cup; a problem exacerbated by their players' involvement in Pacific Islanders internationals.

They will find themselves in a pool alongside England and South Africa once again in 2007. The outcome may well be the same as in 2003, but rest assured, Samoa's reputation for producing world-class players will remain very much intact.

COACH
Michael Jones
The former legendary All Black flanker, who played in the 1987 World Cup-winning side and who was as famous for his unflinching Christian beliefs as for his dynamism on the field of play, returned to his native Samoa as assistant coach to John Boe in 2000. He took over the reins as national coach in 2004.

 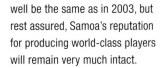

STAR PLAYER: Lome Fa'atua

Position: Winger
Born: 23 October 1975, Wellington, New Zealand
Club: Wellington Hurricanes
Height: 183cm **Weight:** 92kg
Caps: 20 **Points:** 25 (5t)
Debut: v. Fiji, 3 June 2000, Apia

New Zealand-born and recognized as much for the tattoos that cover his legs as for his electric and elusive running, Fa'atua was a star basketball player before he discovered the game of rugby. Joining the Hurricanes in 1999, he made his Samoa debut against Fiji the following year and appeared in the 2003 World Cup, scoring one try but impressing everybody with his searing pace. In 2006 he finally put aside his club journeyman tag with some standout performances in the Super 14 competition as the Hurricanes reached the final and their Samoan winger finished as the tournament's leading try scorer with an impressive tally of ten tries in just 14 appearances. He has also represented the combined Pacific Islanders side.

PLAYING STRIP

Blue shirts with red and white trim, blue shorts and blue socks

FORM SINCE 2003 RUGBY WORLD CUP

Played:	18
Won:	6
Lost:	12
Drawn:	0
Winning percentage:	33.3%
Points for:	487
Points against:	637
Biggest victory:	91–0 v. Barbados, 1 July 2006 at Santa Clara
Heaviest defeat:	77–3 v. Wales, 4 June 2005 at Hartford
Points scored per match:	27.1
Points conceded per match:	35.4

PAST WORLD CUP PERFORMANCES

1987	Group stages
1991	Group stages
1995	Did not qualify
1999	Group stages
2003	Group stages

COACH
Peter Thorburn

A former New Zealand A and Under-21 coach, Peter Thorburn steered the All Blacks to success in the 1989 Hong Kong Sevens. Initially appointed to guide the Eagles to the World Cup, once qualification was gained, the US Rugby Board's first step was to secure Thorburn's services for the tournament proper.

USA

EAGLES STILL WAITING TO SOAR

USA Rugby's mission statement is: "To be a world power both on the field and off the field". The stark reality is that the Eagles have struggled with the tag of being one of the world's rugby minnows and they are still struggling to find the right formula to enable them to join rugby's world elite.

On the four occasions rugby was played in the Olympic Games, the USA took top honours twice, winning gold in both 1920 and 1924. After the latter victory the sport was dropped from the Olympic agenda and, as a result, American interest in rugby waned.

It went through something of a renaissance in the 1960s and '70s and, following an invitation to appear in the inaugural World Cup in 1987, the USA became a member of the IRB. They showed signs of potential in an opening win over Japan (21–18), but losses to both Australia (47–12) and England (34–6) – they were outclassed in both matches – showed that American rugby still had a long way to go.

The perception did not change four years later. They lost all three of their group games to finish bottom of the pile. And the disappointment of missing out on South Africa in 1995 was hardly eased when they returned to the tournament four years later: they suffered three straight defeats, including a morale-crushing 27–25 loss to Romania.

They arrived in Australia in 2003 with low expectations. After losing out narrowly to Fiji in their opening game 19–18 and suffering a hard-fought defeat to Scotland (29–15), they won their first World Cup match for 16 years when they beat Japan 39–26. They bowed out of the tournament, following a battling 41–14 defeat to France, with their heads held high.

Problems always arise for international teams who lack a strong domestic set-up. The USA is no different: the national team has played just 19 internationals since the last World Cup. And despite notching up six victories – including two comfortable victories over Uruguay in their World Cup qualifier play-off – they have struggled every time they played one of the game's major nations.

STAR PLAYER: Paul Emerick

Position: Full-back, centre, winger
Born: 24 January 1980
Club: Newport Gwent Dragons
Height: 183cm **Weight:** 91kg
Caps: 23 **Points:** 35 (7t)
Debut: v. Spain, 12 April 2003, Madrid

Now plying his trade outside the country of his birth, Paul Emerick did not even pick up a rugby ball until he was 19. But the former American footballer and wrestler soon found the game to his liking and, after a string of impressive performances for Chicago, made his international debut just four years later against Spain. He moved to Italian side Amatori in 2004 and the following year moved to Parma, where he played a part in helping his team become the first Italian side to win a game in the Heineken Cup. His powerful performances for Parma earned him a move to the Celtic League side Newport Gwent Dragons – a club he had helped to eliminate from the Heineken Cup in 2005 – in the summer of 2006.

POOL A
SEA EAGLES

POOL A
SEA EAGLES

PLAYING STRIP

Red shirts with white trim, white shorts, red socks

FORM SINCE 2003 RUGBY WORLD CUP

Played:	14
Won:	5
Lost:	9
Drawn:	0
Winning percentage:	35.7%
Points for:	458
Points against:	353
Biggest victory:	90–0 v. Cook Islands, 8 July 2006 at Nuku'alofa
Heaviest defeat:	48–0 v. Italy, 12 November 2005 at Prato
Points scored per match:	32.7
Points conceded per match:	25.2

PAST WORLD CUP PERFORMANCES

1987	Group stages
1991	Group stages
1995	Did not qualify
1999	Group stages
2003	Group stages

COACH
Adam Leach

After a successful coaching stint in Japan, the former New South Wales and Harlequins player replaced Willie Ofahenguae as Tonga's coach in May 2006. He led the Sea Eagles to wins over Fiji and Japan, lifted the side to 16th in the world rankings and secured their qualification for the 2007 World Cup with wins over the Cook Islands and Korea.

TONGA

AS TOUGH AS THEY COME

Although rugby arrived in the region in 1920, it wasn't until 1986 that Tongan rugby finally registered on the European radar. And what an impact, quite literally, they made. From that moment on, Tonga's reputation as rugby's hard men was secure.

Wales were the summer visitors to the Pacific Islands that year and their game against Tonga ended in a mass brawl – involving every player on the pitch, bar two – after the Dragons' flanker Mark Brown was flattened by three Tongan forwards.

So Wales would have been less than delighted when, following Tonga's invite to the inaugural World Cup in 1987, they were paired together in the same group. But despite Wales putting out a second-string XV – no doubt to protect their players – Tonga lost 29–16. Further defeats against Ireland (32–9) and Canada (37–4) meant that Tonga's interest in the tournament came to a premature end.

After failing to qualify for the 1991 competition, they edged out Fiji on points difference to take their place in the 1995 World Cup in South Africa. After losing their first two games – against France (38–10) and Scotland (41–5) – they notched up their first World Cup win against the Ivory Coast. It was, however, a game tinged with tragedy: after just two minutes Ivorian winger Max Brito lay prone on the ground and paralysed. A victory it may have been, but this was no time to celebrate.

They notched up another victory four years later, surprising Italy 28–25, before the physicality of their play came under the spotlight once again. This time England were on the receiving end of some in-your-face Tongan play and prop Ngalu Taufo'ou received his marching orders after knocking England flanker Richard Hill out cold. England won the game and Tonga returned home under a cloud.

Four straight defeats in 2003, including a 91–7 thrashing at the hands of New Zealand, would have done little to lift the gloom.

They were forced to qualify the hard way this time round, via the playoffs, eventually seeing off Korea in the repechage round, and will be looking to their matches against Samoa and the USA to record that third World Cup win.

STAR PLAYER: NILI LATU

Position: Flanker
Born: 19 February 1982, Tongatapu, Tonga
Club: Wellington Hurricanes
Height: 185cm **Weight:** 90kg
Caps: 6 **Points:** 5 (1t)
Debut: v. Japan, 5 June 2006, Fukuoaka

One of the rising stars of Tongan rugby, Nili Latu is an uncompromising, turbo-charged flanker who made a name for himself over the past four seasons playing for the Bay of Plenty in New Zealand's domestic competition. His performances earned him selection for the Wellington Hurricanes in the southern hemisphere's Super 14 competition, primarily as cover for Jerry Collins and Rodney So'oialo. He made his debut for Tonga against Japan in June 2006 and went on to captain the side in their World Cup qualifying victory over the Cook Islands. He has also represented the Pacific Islanders team.

 # AUSTRALIA

PLAYING STRIP

Gold shirts with green trim, green shorts, green socks

FORM SINCE 2003 RUGBY WORLD CUP

Played:	38
Won:	21
Lost:	16
Drawn:	1
Winning percentage:	55.3%
Points for:	1,062
Points against:	759
Biggest victory:	74–7 v. Samoa, 11 June 2005 at Sydney
Heaviest defeat:	32–12 v. New Zealand, 3 September 2005 at Christchurch
Points scored per match:	27.9
Points conceded per match:	19.9

PAST WORLD CUP PERFORMANCES

1987	Semi-finals
1991	CHAMPIONS
1995	Quarter-finals
1999	CHAMPIONS
2003	Runners-up

Matt Giteau: Although he was named as one of the five best players in the world in 2004, the Wallabies are still trying to work out how to get the best out of the immensely talented player who is equally at home in the half-back line or in the centres.

DEFYING THE ODDS

Australia are the only team to have lifted the World Cup twice, a remarkable achievement for a nation with relatively few rugby players – only 140,000 out of a population of 20 million. What's more, they have also managed to produce some of the greatest players ever to have stepped on to a rugby pitch.

Given their success in the World Cup, it was somewhat ironic that the greatest side Australia ever produced never got its hands on the greatest prize in the game. Having created a fearsome reputation following a Grand Slam tour of the Home Nations in 1984 and a 2–1 away series win over the All Blacks in 1986, Mark Ella, David Campese, Nick Farr-Jones and co., all playing at their peak, entered the inaugural World Cup in 1987 as strong favourites. And they stuck closely to the pre-tournament script until France upset the apple cart, with Serge Blanco crossing the line in the last minute to secure a dramatic 30–24 victory to break Australian hearts.

They regrouped and went into the 1991 tournament with both a new attitude and a new coach, Bob Dwyer. But their smooth progress through the group stages almost came to a shuddering halt against Ireland in

Dublin in the quarter-finals. With just seconds remaining on the clock and with Ireland holding a slender 18–15 lead, Michael Lynagh crashed over the line to keep Wallaby hopes alive. Their confidence duly restored, they produced some scintillating rugby against New Zealand in the semi-finals to race into a 13–3 half-time lead and showed their defensive mettle in the second half to win 16–6. It was a similar pattern in the final: they scored an early try to take the lead and repelled wave after wave of England attacks to hold out for a 12–6 victory. Australia were the champions of the world.

They never looked like retaining their crown four years later. An opening-game 27–18 defeat to South Africa condemned them to second place in the pool and a quarter-final clash against England. It was a dramatic game: neck and neck entering the final moments of the

match, England fly-half Rob Andrew's last-gasp drop-goal brought Australia's interest in the tournament to a premature end.

It was a new generation of Wallabies who travelled to Europe in 1999. Led by John Eales, the likes of George Gregan, Matt Burke and Joe Roff were seldom threatened. Pulse rates may have risen during their tense 27–21 semi-final victory over South Africa, but the final in Cardiff was an altogether more comfortable affair as Australia cruised to a 35–12 victory over an exhausted France to become the first nation to lift the trophy twice.

As hosts, four years later, they came agonizingly close to securing a hat-trick of titles. Playing indifferent rugby they finished on top of their pool before easing to a 33–16 win over Scotland in the quarter-finals. Then they produced their best performance of the competition, shocking New Zealand 22–10 in the last four to book their final place. And, in front of a passionate home crowd, they almost produced another upset in the Final, pushing England into extra-time before falling to Jonny Wilkinson's last-minute drop-goal.

Post-World Cup wins over Scotland and a 51–15 thrashing of England would have done much to put a smile back on the face of Australian rugby, but it did not last long. They won only one of their four games in a disappointing 2004 Tri Nations campaign. It should not have come as much of a surprise: Eales, Burke and Ben Tune among others had all departed the scene and the void they left was proving difficult to fill.

The Wallabies' form continued to dip through 2005. Victories over Samoa, Italy and France were followed by seven straight defeats and, although they stopped the rot with a 30–14 win over Ireland, a 24–22 defeat to Wales a week later was the final straw. Eddie Jones, the man who had coached them to the World Cup final just two years earlier, was sacked and George Gregan was stripped of the captaincy.

The Wallabies' hierarchy turned to John Connolly to arrest the nation's declining rugby fortunes. He got off to a great start, notching up wins over England and Ireland, but any real progress would have been measured against their performances in the 2006 Tri Nations campaign. They got off to a nightmare start, crashing to a 32–12 reverse against New Zealand in Christchurch, but rallied well to win two of their final three games. That was followed by an indifferent tour to Europe, where the frustration of a 29–29 draw with Wales and the pain of a 21–6 defeat to an in-form Ireland would have tempered any joy felt as a result of victories over Italy and Scotland.

Australia have won the World Cup every time it has been staged in the northern hemisphere and, although the odds are very much against them repeating the feat this time round, you can never count the Wallabies out. They seem to be a team that enjoys defying the rugby odds.

STAR PLAYER: Lote Tuqiri

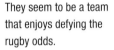

Position: Winger, centre
Born: 23 September 1979, Namatakula, Fiji
Club: Warratahs
Height: 191cm *Weight:* 103kg
Caps: 50 *Points:* 125 (25t)
Debut: v. Ireland, 7 June 2003, Perth

One of a growing number of players to have represented his country at both rugby union and league, Lote Tuqiri made his name with the Brisbane Broncos and Queensland between 1999 and 2001. He captained Fiji in the 2000 Rugby League World Cup and was picked for Australia the following year. After switching codes in 2002, he made his international debut against Ireland in Perth a year later. He has since gone on to become one of the most clinical finishers in the game and has been employed on both the wing and at outside-centre. Speculation about his future is rife, with many believing he will switch back to league following the 2007 World Cup.

PLAYING STRIP

Red shirts with white trim, white shorts, red socks

FORM SINCE 2003 RUGBY WORLD CUP

Played:	40
Won:	19
Lost:	19
Drawn:	2
Winning percentage:	47.5%
Points for:	1,187
Points against:	939
Biggest victory:	98–0 v. Japan, 26 November 2004 at Cardiff
Heaviest defeat:	53–18 v. South Africa, 26 June 2004 at Pretoria
Points scored per match:	29.7
Points conceded per match:	23.5

PAST WORLD CUP PERFORMANCES

1987	Semi-finals
1991	Group stages
1995	Group stages
1999	Quarter-finals
2003	Quarter-finals

Martyn Williams: The Welsh flanker is undoubtedly one of the most underrated performers in world rugby. When Williams is at his best, so usually are Wales.

WALES

WORLD CUP UNDERACHIEVERS

If passion for the game alone were enough to claim the World Cup then Wales would have been multiple winners of the trophy. As it is, their record in the tournament has left their diehard fans in the valleys with little to sing about and it would be a major surprise if they reversed that trend in 2007.

Not that many Welsh rugby fans were feeling that way following the inaugural World Cup in 1987. They departed the tournament as the third best team in the world after clinching a dramatic third-place play-off victory over Australia. In some respects, it was the worst thing that could have happened to Welsh rugby; that performance masked the fact that, in reality, they had fallen a long way behind the southern hemisphere teams.

Their march to the semi-finals had been straightforward: they found themselves in the last four having barely been stretched in either the group stages or the quarter-finals, where they brushed aside a misfiring England 16–3. Their reward was a match-up against New Zealand for a place in the final and the manner of their 49–6 defeat should have set alarm bells

ringing. Instead, Paul Thorburn's last-gasp conversion to win the play-off game against Australia remained the talking point throughout Wales. The fact that their opponents had suffered a morale-crushing defeat to France in their own semi-final and clearly were not interested in a play-off game was conveniently ignored.

But as good as the mood had been post-1987, it could not have been blacker following the 1991 tournament. Wales never recovered from a shock opening 16–13 loss to Western Samoa and were summarily dismissed from the competition following a 38–3 walloping at the hands of Australia. Welsh rugby was at an all-time low.

And things barely improved four years later in South Africa. As a result of their poor showing in the previous tournament, Wales found themselves in a

tough pool alongside New Zealand, Ireland and Japan. A comfortable victory over Japan in their opening game was followed by a creditable performance in their 34–9 defeat against New Zealand and hopes were high for their winner-takes-all encounter against Ireland in their final pool match. They lost, 24–23, and suffered their second early tournament exit in a row.

Graham Henry's appointment as coach in 1998 re-galvanized Welsh rugby and they entered the 1999 tournament, as hosts, full of confidence. Although the Samoans again beat Wales in the last pool game, this time it made little difference; with wins over Argentina 23–18 and Japan 64–15, Wales topped the group on points difference and took their place in the quarter-finals. But Wales's involvement ended there, Australia proving too strong for them in a 24–9 victory in Cardiff. Still, things seemed to be on the up.

And that feeling was confirmed in 2003. Although Henry had departed, Wales opened their campaign by winning three straight pool games before losing the last one to New Zealand, 53–37, but their performance against the All Blacks gave them great heart for their last-eight clash against England. And for the first hour of that quarter-final, it seemed a major upset was on the cards, but England showed the reserves that took them to the world crown and scratched out a 28–17 victory.

It wasn't until two years later that Wales re-emerged as a true force in world rugby. Now coached by Mike Ruddock, they opened their 2005 Six Nations campaign with a nerve-racking 11–9 victory over England. After brushing aside the attentions of Italy in their next game, they arrived in Paris for a showdown against France with their confidence high and produced some breathtaking rugby to emerge 24–18 winners. A comfortable 46–22 win over Scotland at Murrayfield set up a grand-slam encounter against Ireland in front of a capacity Millennium Stadium crowd. Wales did not disappoint, running out 32–20 winners to record their first Grand Slam in 28 years.

They opened their autumn campaign with a much-hyped clash against New Zealand, but it was one-way traffic as the All Blacks romped to a 41–3 victory; Wales's worst-ever loss on home soil. They lost again to South Africa and, by the time they entered the 2006 Six Nations – with a number of their 2005 heroes on the long-term injury list – a few cracks were starting to appear in their armour.

And those cracks became canyons following the shock resignation of Ruddock after the second game. A disrupted Wales ended a sorry campaign with one win, one draw and three defeats to their name and stuck at fifth place in the table.

A 29–29 draw against Australia was the highlight of their 2006 autumn campaign and although the 2007 Six Nations saw the return to action of many of the old guard, the team's performances would have done little to raise morale. They remain woefully out of form going into the 2007 World Cup.

 STAR PLAYER: Ryan Jones

Position: *No.8/flanker*
Born: *13 March 1981, Newport, Wales*
Club: *Ospreys*
Height: *196cm* **Weight:** *114kg*
Caps: *11* **Points:** *5 (1t)*
Debut: *v. South Africa, 6 November 2004, Cardiff*

Ryan Jones was a goalkeeper with Bristol City until the age of 14. He switched to the Ospreys in 2004 after his previous team, the Celtic Warriors, had gone bust, and it signalled the start of a sensational 12 months for the back-row star. He made his debut for Wales in November that year, helped the Ospreys to the Celtic League title, played a crucial role in Wales's 2005 Grand Slam-winning campaign and, as a result, earned a late call-up to the Lions touring party in New Zealand as cover for the injured Simon Jones. He put in a scintillating display during the Lions' 30–19 victory over Otago and went on to play a part in all three Tests. He returned widely considered the star of what had otherwise been a disappointing tour. Shoulder surgery set him back in 2005, but as Wales launch their assault on the 2007 World Cup, he looks to be back to his best.

PLAYING STRIP

White shirts with black and blue trim, black shorts, black socks

FORM SINCE 2003 RUGBY WORLD CUP

Played:	15
Won:	9
Lost:	6
Drawn:	0
Winning percentage:	60.0%
Points for:	305
Points against:	358
Biggest victory:	29–3 v. Samoa, 12 June 2004 in Suva
Heaviest defeat:	91–0 v. New Zealand, 10 June 2005 in Albany
Points scored per match:	20.3
Points conceded per match:	23.9

PAST WORLD CUP PERFORMANCES

1987	Quarter-finals
1991	Group stages
1995	Did not qualify
1999	Quarter-final play-offs
2003	Group stages

FIJI

FUN-LOVING FIJIANS NEED RESULTS

If ever a team captured the heart and soul of the game of rugby, it is Fiji. They thrill rugby audiences with their all-out style of attacking play wherever they go, but although Fiji have dominated the seven-a-side scene for almost three decades, they have always struggled with the 15-a-side version of the game.

After seeing the Fijians outclass the Maoris 14–4 in Hamilton in 1939, a journalist from the *Waikato Times* was moved to write: "Almost uncanny in handling the ball, lightning in the pace of their sprinting, relentless in their dive tackling … and all the time pursuing methods of bright, open football, the Fijians gave a sparkling display and thrilled the large crowd." Many of the same emotions are stirred to this day. The problem is Fiji have always struggled to come to terms with the subtle technicalities of the longer version of the game and, as a result, successes against rugby's elite teams have been limited.

Not that they haven't pulled off the odd shock, none more famous than their 25–21 victory over the British Lions in 1977, but the fact of the matter is, with more than 80,000 registered players out of a population of

850,000 – a figure greater than the likes of Ireland or Wales – Fiji should have done better.

On paper at least, they gave a good account of themselves in the inaugural World Cup in 1987. They lost 74–13 to New Zealand and 18–15 to Italy, but their opening 28–9 win over Argentina, coupled with the South Americans' subsequent victory over the Italians, left them in second place in the pool, courtesy of points difference, and handed them a place in the quarter-finals. The lost out to the French, 31–16. Quarter-finalists they may have been, but they had won only one of their four games in the tournament.

Which was one more than they managed to win four years later in the British Isles. In what was a miserable tournament for the islanders, they slumped to defeats against Canada (13–3), France (33–9) and, hardest to

Moses Rauluni: Brought up in Brisbane and a former Australian youth international, the Saracens scrum-half provides a crucial link between the Fijian pack and their backs.

take of all, Romania (17–15) to depart the World Cup both early and embarrassed. And any disappointment felt at such performances would have increased tenfold when they failed to qualify for the 1995 event in South Africa.

A change in direction was desperately needed if Fiji were to fulfil their undoubted potential. New Zealander Brad Johnstone was brought in as coach in the hope that his experience would help mould the Fijians into a more disciplined unit. It seemed to do the trick. They duly qualified for the 1999 World Cup, where they opened up with fine victories over Namibia (67–18) and Canada (38–22). And many believe they would have completed a hat-trick of wins and won their group had it not been for some dubious decisions by Irish referee Paddy O'Brien in their final pool match against France. In what turned out to be the most dramatic and closely fought tie of the competition, a disallowed Fiji try for a knock-on and a French penalty-try that defied belief proved the difference between the two sides. Defeat condemned Fiji to a quarter-final play-off against England at Twickenham, where they ran out of steam and crashed to a 45–24 defeat.

More bad luck dogged Fiji in 2003, when they missed out on a quarter-final spot after recovering from an opening-game 61–18 defeat to France to edge out the United States (19–18) and Japan (41–13) to set up what was effectively a quarter-final play-off against Scotland. In a close-fought encounter, they lost 22–20 and their

World Cup dreams, albeit by the closest of margins, had been dashed once again.

As is the case with all of the Pacific Island teams, Fiji have paid the price of professional rugby. They have lost the likes of cousins Joe Rokocoko and Sitiveni Sivivatu to New Zealand and Lote Tuqiri to Australia. And with many of their players plying their trade in both the major leagues of the northern and southern hemispheres, getting them all together to train and play internationals has been problematic. By the time the 2007 World Cup comes around, Fiji will have played only 16 internationals since the last tournament.

And the results have proved the same old story for Fijian rugby: dominant over their South Pacific neighbours – in their matches against Samoa and Tonga their record reads played seven, won five, lost two – they have crashed every time they have faced one of the game's big boys, including a thumping 91–0 defeat to New Zealand and an altogether closer 11–10 loss to Wales.

Their preparation for the World Cup was thrown into turmoil by the shock resignation of their New Zealand coach Wayne Pivac in January 2007. Ilivasi Tabua, the former Fiji and Australia international, was named as his replacement and, surprise, surprise, cited his intentions to play fast, running rugby. Expect Fijian victories over Canada and Japan, but it will be their performances against Australia and Wales that determine how far Fiji will progress in the 2007 World Cup.

PLAYERS TO WATCH

Norman Ligairi
Age 31 Position Full-back
Club Brive (Fra) Caps 37
Points 80 (16t)

Moses Luveitasau
Age 27 Position Wing
Club Cardiff Blues Caps 8
Points 20 (4t)

Seru Rabeni
Age 29 Position Centre/wing
Club Leicester Tigers Caps 21
Points 5 (1t)

Kameli Ratuvou
Age 23 Position Centre
Club Saracens Caps 8
Points 15 (3t)

Moses Rauluni
Age 32 Position Scrum-half
Club Saracens Caps 33
Points 5 (1t)

COACH
Ilivasi Tabua

Having played 11 Tests for Australia and 17 times for his native Fiji, the man nicknamed the "Human Skewer" during his illustrious playing career for his all-action style of tackling moved from his position of assistant coach to national coach following the shock resignation of Wayne Pivac in January 2007.

 STAR PLAYER: Rupeni Caucaunibuca

Position: Winger
Born: 5 June 1980, Fiji
Club: Agen (Fra)
Height: 180cm **Weight:** 105kg
Caps: 9 **Points:** 45 (9t)
Debut: v. France, 11 October 2003, Brisbane

Rupeni Caucaunibuca is as controversial as he is talented. After a string of glittering performances in the 2003 World Cup – in which he scored two tries – he announced his intention to quit Fiji to play for New Zealand. He may have recanted on that decision, but he sparked more controversy when he missed Fiji's World Cup qualifying game against Samoa in 2005 claiming his wife had an infected tooth. The Fiji Rugby Union weren't prepared to run with the story and promptly banned him for a year. He returned in style, scoring a try as Fiji recorded a 29–18 win over Italy. He has been the top try scorer in French domestic rugby for the past two seasons, Player of the Year in 2006, and many rugby pundits consider him to be the most devastating player in world rugby.

PLAYING STRIP
Red shirts with black and white trim, black shorts, black socks

FORM SINCE 2003 RUGBY WORLD CUP
Played:	17
Won:	7
Lost:	10
Drawn:	0
Winning percentage:	41.2%
Points for:	378
Points against:	569
Biggest victory:	69–3 v. Barbados, 24 June 2006 at Bridgetown
Heaviest defeat:	70–0 v. England, 13 November 2004 at Twickenham
Points scored per match:	22.2
Points conceded per match:	33.5

PAST WORLD CUP PERFORMANCES
1987	Group stages
1991	Quarter-finals
1995	Group stages
1999	Group stages
2003	Group stages

COACH
Ric Suggitt

A former coach of the national women's team, head coach of the Under-23 Academy and the coach of Canada's sevens team since 1999, Ric Suggitt, a former full-back at provincial level, took charge of the national side in February 2004 and successfully guided Canada into their sixth successive World Cup.

CANADA

STUCK AT FIRST BASE

Not so long ago, Canada were poised to take their place among rugby's world elite. They had just made it to the quarter-finals of the World Cup and possessed players of genuine class, but their game seems to have regressed in recent years and they remain a team on the periphery of the world's elite.

Having been part of the international rugby scene since the 1930s, it was only natural that Canada should have been one of the invitees to the inaugural World Cup in 1987. And although they suffered defeats against Ireland (46–19) and Wales (40–9), their comprehensive 37–4 victory over Tonga in their final game more than justified the invite.

It was a far better Canadian team that travelled to the British Isles in 1991. Bolstered by the emergence of world-class players such as Gareth Rees, "Stormin'" Norm Hadley and Al Charron, they beat Fiji (13–3) and Romania (19–11) in their opening two games. A narrow defeat to France, 19–13, left them second in their pool and facing a tough quarter-final tie against New Zealand. They put in a valiant display, but went down 29–13. This quarter-final exit remains Canada's best World Cup performance.

Four years later, when the World Cup switched to South Africa, Canada found themselves in a tricky group alongside the hosts, defending champions Australia and Romania. They beat the latter in their opening game, 34–3, but then came the disappointment of two defeats, 27–11 to the Wallabies and 20–0 to South Africa, the latter being a tense game that saw two Canadians given their marching orders.

A 73–11 victory over Namibia four years later came too late to ease the pain of earlier defeats to France (23–20) and a resurgent Fiji (38–22) and in many ways it was a tournament of huge significance for the Canucks: their failure to qualify for the last eight for the second tournament in a row showed that their rugby fortunes had taken a downward turn.

There was little to cheer about in 2003 either. Just as had been the case in 1987, a 24–7 victory over Tonga was Canada's only one of the tournament and drawn in a tough group this time of asking, it's difficult to see them going any better in France 2007.

 STAR PLAYER: James Pritchard

Position: Full-back/wing
Born: 21 July 1979, Parkes, New South Wales, Australia
Club: Northampton Saints
Height: 175 cm **Weight:** 85kg
Caps: 9 **Points:** 129 (8t, 22c, 15p)
Debut: v. NZ Maoris, 26 July 2003, Calgary

A former rugby league player in his native Australia, he switched to rugby union with Randwick and picked up the most improved player award in 2000. Moving to Bedford in England's Division One, he broke the league's scoring record in 2003 with 374 points and was voted player of the year. Qualified to play for Canada through his grandfather, he made his debut against the NZ Maoris in 2003 and took his place in Canada's line-up at the 2003 World Cup. He came to the fore during Canada's 2007 World Cup qualifying campaign, scoring a national record 26 points against Barbados and improved on it by contributing a massive 36 points in the crunch game against the United States. He has played for the English Premiership club Northampton Saints since January 2006.

35

JAPAN

PLAYING STRIP
Dark red shirts with white hoops, black shorts, black socks

FORM SINCE 2003 RUGBY WORLD CUP

Played:	26
Won:	11
Lost:	14
Drawn:	1
Winning percentage:	42.3%
Points for:	745
Points against:	815
Biggest victory:	82–9 v. Arabian Gulf, 16 April 2006 in Tokyo
Heaviest defeat:	100–8 v. Scotland, 13 November 2004 in Perth (Aus)
Points scored per match:	28.7
Points conceded per match:	31.3

PAST WORLD CUP PERFORMANCES

1987	Group stages
1991	Group stages
1995	Group stages
1999	Group stages
2003	Group stages

COACH
John Kirwan
The legendary former All Black winger made his name as a coach when in charge of the Italian national side from 2002 to 2005. Under his tutelage, the *Azzurri* made great progress. However, he was relieved from his post following a winless campaign in the 2005 Six Nations. He took over at the helm of Japanese rugby on 1 January 2007.

CHERRY BLOSSOMS SEEK IMPROVEMENT

Japan is the only Asian nation to have appeared in every World Cup and have the fourth largest number of registered players in the world, but that is where the good news ends. They may be the dominant team in South East Asia, but they have always struggled on the game's biggest stage.

The Cherry Blossoms' World Cup record reads like a horror story: they have won just one of their 16 games – against Zimbabwe, 54–0 at Lansdowne Road in 1991 – and have taken some heavy beatings along the way, none worse than the 145–17 hammering at the hands of a second-string New Zealand team out to prove a point at the 1995 World Cup in South Africa. Japan leaked 21 tries that day, a result which was a hammer blow for the game's popularity back home.

But Japan is a proud nation with a 108-year history of the game. They may have taken further beatings at the 1999 World Cup, but when they thrashed Taiwan 155–3 in a World Cup qualifying game in 2002, they went a long way to banishing the ghosts of Bloemfontein 1995 and could finally escape the shackles of that defeat.

They departed the 2003 World Cup in Australia having thrilled the crowds with some entertaining, fast-flowing rugby and hailed as the best of the so-called minnows, but they still failed to win a game and suffered disappointing defeats to Fiji (41–13) and the United States (39–26).

Japan's post-World Cup performances have stuck to the formbook. They remain the dominant force in Asian rugby but continue to struggle when they play teams from other parts of the world, the low point coming when they found themselves on the wrong end of a 98–0 hammering against Wales in the Millennium Stadium in November 2004.

Having secured qualification for the 2007 edition of the tournament with some ease, they pulled off something of a coup by recruiting the services of former Italy coach John Kirwan. The former All Black has set wins over Canada and Fiji as Japan's major World Cup objective: they haven't beaten the Pacific Islanders for 13 years, although their record against Canada is altogether more encouraging – they last beat the Canucks in 2004.

 STAR PLAYER: Daisuke Ohata

Position: Wing/centre
Born: 11 November 1975, Osaka, Japan
Club: Kobe Steel Kobelco
Height: 176cm **Weight:** 80kg
Caps: 55 **Points:** 325 (65t)
Debut: v. Korea, 9 November 1996, Tokyo

Japan may not be one of the superpowers of world rugby, but they possess the most prolific try scorer ever to have played the game. On 14 May 2006, Daisuke Ohata scored three tries in Japan's victory over Georgia to take his tally to 65 tries in 55 Tests and past David Campese's world record that had stood for a decade. He broke on to the scene at the 1999 Hong Kong Sevens, a spawning ground for the game's biggest names, and was voted as the tournament's most valuable player – an accolade once awarded to Campese. At that year's World Cup he served notice of his searing speed with a spectacular try against Wales. And, eight years later, still the tries continue to come.

PLAYING STRIP

Black shirts, black shorts, black socks

FORM SINCE 2003 RUGBY WORLD CUP

Played:	38
Won:	34
Lost:	4
Drawn:	0
Winning percentage:	89.5%
Points for:	1,336
Points against:	596
Biggest victory:	91–0 v. Fiji, 10 June 2005 at Albany
Heaviest defeat:	40–26 v. South Africa, 14 August 2004 at Johannesburg
Points scored per match:	35.2
Points conceded per match:	15.7

PAST WORLD CUP PERFORMANCES

1987	CHAMPIONS
1991	Semi-finals
1995	Runners-up
1999	Semi-finals
2003	Semi-finals

NEW ZEALAND

WORLD CUP SUCCESS IS LONG OVERDUE

Winners of more World Cup games than any other team, the major surprise is that New Zealand have only once got their hands on the game's greatest prize. However, the All Blacks enter the 2007 tournament as firm favourites and full of hope that their 20-year wait for the world championship is set to come to an end.

Even when they won the tournament it came as a surprise. The 1987 New Zealand team was a side in turmoil entering the inaugural World Cup in their own backyard. It came on the back of an unsuccessful 1986 season while the country was still reeling from the fall-out from an unofficial New Zealand tour to South Africa which had seen several of their star players banned. What's more, disenfranchised by the state of their team, the New Zealand public were turning their backs on their heroes in droves.

The All Blacks slowly started to win them back. They won their pool comfortably, proved too much for Scotland to win their quarter-final 30–3 and thumped Wales 49–6 to take their place in the final in front of a now-adoring Eden Park crowd. Then, in what turned out to be a happy day for an entire country, the All

Blacks ran in three tries to France's one en route to a comfortable 29–9 victory. New Zealand were the champions of the world.

But it was an ageing team that travelled to the northern hemisphere four years later. Even though they topped their pool with three victories, including a comfortable win over England at Twickenham, a less than convincing 29–13 win over a resilient Canada in the quarter-finals showed cracks in the New Zealand armour. Australia duly exposed them, running out 16–6 winners in the semi-final at Lansdowne Road. It proved the end of the line for a large number of this New Zealand team.

New coach Laurie Mains spent the interim four years blooding a new generation of All Black stars. By the time the 1995 World Cup in South Africa came around,

Richie McCaw: The current IRB Player of the Year, the New Zealand captain is a dynamic open-side flanker who literally leads from the front.

young guns Jeff Wilson, Josh Kronfeld and Andrew Mehrtens were taking the rugby world by storm. But it was their youngest player of all who was stealing all the headlines. Their giant winger Jonah Lomu left opponent after opponent in his wake – he scored four tries against England in the semi-final in Cape Town – as New Zealand marched impressively through the tournament to reach the final against South Africa.

Mystery and speculation abound around events leading up to the 1995 World Cup final. Somehow, somewhere, the New Zealand squad went down with a bout of food poisoning the day before what would be the biggest match of their careers. And they seemed a shadow of their former selves on the day itself, never getting into their stride and losing out 15–12 in a disappointing game that amounted to little more than a kicking contest. While a jubilant South Africa was left dancing in the streets, a shell-shocked New Zealand squad was left to wonder where it had all gone wrong.

With many of the team out to avenge the disappointments of 1995, New Zealand marched through their pool imperiously when the World Cup returned to Europe in 1999. And, despite a wobble in the quarter-finals – a nervy New Zealand struggled to a 30–18 victory over Scotland – the All Blacks remained strong favourites to overcome France in the semi-finals. The French had different ideas, however, producing half an hour of scintillating second-half rugby to come from behind and secure an unforgettable, and from an

All Black perspective, bitterly disappointing 43–31 win. Their long wait for World Cup glory was set to continue.

Many believed it would come to an end in 2003. New Zealand entered the fifth World Cup on the back of an unbeaten Tri Nations campaign – one that saw them win the Bledisloe Cup for the first time since 1998 – and full of confidence. They eased through their pool matches once again, with only Wales pushing them beyond first gear, gained some measure of revenge over South Africa in the quarter-finals with a 29–9 victory, and faced up to their semi-final against Australia in the full knowledge that they had already beaten the Wallabies twice that year. Australia ignored the formbook, playing their best rugby of the tournament to run out 22–10 winners. The All Blacks were reeling.

They appointed Graham Henry to the task of taking New Zealand to World Cup glory. And what a fist of it he has made. With the exceptional Dan Carter steering the All Black ship from fly-half, and under the inspirational leadership of 2006 IRB Player of the Year Richie McCaw, New Zealand have lost just three times since the last World Cup, on each occasion to South Africa in South Africa. Along the way they have pummelled their opponents into submission, including a British Lions touring side that contained many of England's 2003 World Cup-winning team. The All Blacks will travel to France with the strongest pool of players on the planet. They have been in this position before and failed; this time nothing short of success will do.

COACH
Graham Henry
Following a hugely successful spell with Auckland between 1992 and 1997, Graham Henry, having missed out on the All Black coaching post, took charge of Wales and helped revive the country's flagging rugby fortunes. He became the New Zealand coach following the 2003 World Cup and led the All Blacks to Tri Nations success in both 2005 and 2006. Only World Cup success is missing from his hugely impressive CV.

STAR PLAYER: Dan Carter

Position: Fly-half
Born: 5 March 1982, Canterbury, New Zealand
Club: Canterbury Crusaders
Height: 178cm **Weight:** 91kg
Caps: 35 **Points:** 540 (16t, 98c, 87p, 1dg)
Debut: v. Wales, 21 June 2003, Hamilton

The star of the 2002 Under-21 World Championship in South Africa, Dan Carter made his debut for both the Canterbury Crusaders and New Zealand the following year. He found himself on the bench as the All Blacks floundered at the 2003 World Cup, where their lack of a consistent goal-kicker cost them dear, but it worked to his advantage and by 2004 he had established his place in the All Blacks' starting line-up. However, it was his performance in the second Test against the British Lions that set tongues wagging: he finished the game with 33 points and had firmly established his legend as the best fly-half in the world. He was voted the 2005 IRB International Player of the Year.

PLAYING STRIP

Blue shirts with white trim, blue shorts, blue socks

FORM SINCE 2003 RUGBY WORLD CUP

Played:	39
Won:	13
Lost:	26
Drawn:	0
Winning percentage:	33.3%
Points for:	868
Points against:	987
Biggest victory:	100–8 v. Japan, 13 November 2004, Perth (Aus)
Heaviest defeat:	46–22 v. Wales, 13 March 2005 at Murrayfield
Points scored per match:	22.3
Points conceded per match:	25.3

PAST WORLD CUP PERFORMANCES

1987	Quarter-finals
1991	Semi-finals
1995	Quarter-finals
1999	Quarter-finals
2003	Quarter-finals

Jason White: Injury robbed Scotland of their talismanic leader during the 2007 Six Nations, but expect him to be fit and raring to go for the World Cup. Scotland will welcome him back with open arms...

SCOTLAND

PASSION AND PRIDE

With fewer players to choose from than either Tonga or Samoa, Scotland's impact on world rugby is nothing short of sensational. Through a combination of passion, pride and an uncanny ability to punch well above their weight, Scotland came to the 1987 World Cup as an established force among rugby's world elite.

And they arrived with some confidence, too. After all, they were 13-time winners of the then Five Nations tournament, had stormed to the Grand Slam in 1984 and were joint winners in 1986. And they got off to a great start as well, drawing 20–20 with reigning Five Nations champions France in their opening game.

But although comfortable victories over Zimbabwe and Romania followed, the French managed to do even better against the two rugby minnows and topped the group courtesy of points difference. Second place in the group condemned Scotland to a quarter-final match-up against New Zealand. The Scots crashed to a 30–3 defeat and their interest in the inaugural World Cup was over.

They fared much better in Europe four years later. A crucial 24–15 victory over Ireland in their final pool match secured top spot and their reward was a quarter-final clash – in every sense of the word – against Western Samoa. Bloodied and bruised the Scots may have been as they left the Murrayfield pitch after the game, but they were wearing a huge collective smile on their faces following a 28–6 victory. Next up were England at Murrayfield.

Having beaten the Auld Enemy a year earlier at the same venue in a dramatic Five Nations Grand Slam showdown, it was a game the Scots would have approached with huge confidence, but they were stunned by Rob Andrew's last-minute drop-goal. England won 9–6 and Scottish hearts were broken.

Following the pattern of eight years earlier, France pipped Scotland to the top of the pool in South Africa in 1995. And, as had been the case in 1987, Scotland's penalty was a quarter-final match against New Zealand, a team that was fast becoming Scotland's World Cup nemesis. And this was an All

Black side with a difference: they possessed arguably the most destructive player the rugby world has ever seen – Jonah Lomu, who was at his peak and cutting swathes through the tournament. Scotland lost out 48–30. The only consolation was that they managed to restrict the giant winger to just one try.

The Scots had to settle for second place in the pool once again when the World Cup returned to the northern hemisphere in 1999. Although they entered the tournament as Five Nations champions, it came as little surprise that South Africa had managed to claim top spot in the Scots' pool: it came as even less of a surprise that, having ended Samoan hopes in a quarter-final play-off, Scotland's opponents in the last eight – for the third time in four World Cups – would be New Zealand. And it wasn't third time lucky, either: the All Blacks were too much for Scotland and ran out 30–18 winners.

It was a similar pattern for the Scots when they headed down under in 2003. Second place in the pool stages left them with another tricky quarter-final clash, not against New Zealand, but against Australia. The result was the same: the Wallabies won 33–16 and Scotland were sent packing from the World Cup at the quarter-final stage for the third tournament in a row.

Then the wheels seemed to fall off Scottish rugby. Scotland appointed their first foreign coach, Matt Williams, in December 2003 and went on to suffer a miserable Six Nations campaign, where they lost all five matches and ended up with the wooden spoon. They

only managed to win one match in the following year's Six Nations, 13–10 against Italy in Rome, at the end of which Williams's record made ugly reading: played 12, won 2, lost 10. The Australian may well have forged a young, new team of his own making, but in a world where results matter, that was never going to be enough to safeguard his job. Frank Hadden took control for the summer internationals against the Barbarians and Romania. Scotland won them both.

The change of regime triggered a new spirit in Scottish rugby. They opened their 2006 Six Nations account with a shock 20–16 win over France, albeit at home. Another memorable Murrayfield victory, this time 18–12 over England, was sandwiched between away defeats to Wales and Ireland, but when the Scots travelled to Rome and again beat Italy 13–10, it marked the end to what had been a respectable campaign and a significant upturn in fortune.

But injuries to key players marred their autumn 2006 campaign and handicapped them during the 2007 Six Nations, during which they were hammered 37–17 by the Italians – Pool C opponents at the World Cup – at Murrayfield.

Scotland will enjoy home advantage during the World Cup pool stages and you can fully expect their game against the Italians to be the decider for the group's second quarter-final berth. However, it's difficult to see either the Scots or the *Azzurri* challenging the All Blacks' dominance in the pool.

COACH
Frank Hadden

Having taking charge of various Scottish age-group teams, Frank Hadden was appointed as coach of the Edinburgh Gunners in 2000. Four years later he became the first Scottish coach of a Scottish club to take a team to the quarter-finals of the Heineken Cup. The SRU turned to him for the role of national coach in 2005 and he instigated a revival, leading the Scots to three wins and third place in the 2006 Six Nations.

 **STAR PLAYER:** Sean Lamont

Position: *Wing*
Born: *15 January 1981, Perth, Scotland*
Club: *Northampton Saints*
Height: *188cm* **Weight:** *99kg*
Caps: *18* **Points:** *25 (5t)*
Debut: *v. Samoa, 4 June 2004, Wellington*

The former Rotherham player burst on to the domestic rugby scene following his move to Glasgow in 2003. His performances earned him selection for Scotland's 2004 summer tour to Samoa and he marked his first appearance at Murrayfield in Scotland's autumn match against Australia with a try. His Six Nations debut went even better, as an explosive performance in both defence and attack saw him pick up the man of the match award against Italy. His performances during the tournament caught the eye of Northampton Saints and Lamont joined the Midland club in 2005. In 2006, his elusive, powerful running played a major part in Scotland's surprise victories over France (he scored two tries) and England, and during what has been an otherwise disappointing 2007 Six Nations campaign, he has been one of the few Scotland players to consistently catch the eye.

PLAYING STRIP

Light blue shirts, white shorts, light blue socks

FORM SINCE 2003 RUGBY WORLD CUP

Played:	38
Won:	13
Lost:	24
Drawn:	1
Winning percentage:	34.2%
Points for:	883
Points against:	977
Biggest victory:	83–0 v. Portugal, 7 October 2006 in Rome
Heaviest defeat:	69–21 v. Australia, 25 June 2005 in Melbourne
Points scored per match:	23.2
Points conceded per match:	25.7

PAST WORLD CUP PERFORMANCES

1987	Group stages
1991	Group stages
1995	Group stages
1999	Group stages
2003	Group stages

Mauro Bergamasco: A stand-out performer since making his international debut at the age of just 19, the Stade Français flanker is one Italy's few world-class performers.

ITALY

THE *AZZURRI* ARE ON THE UP

Participants in all five World Cups and a proud member of the Six Nations elite, the popularity of rugby in Italy is at an all-time high. But although the *Azzurri* have never made it beyond the group stages of the competition, they will travel to the 2007 World Cup in the best shape they have ever been.

Italy could not have picked a tougher introduction to World Cup rugby. The fixture list matched them against New Zealand in their opening pool game and the All Blacks handed out a harsh rugby lesson, cantering to a 70–6 victory. But the *Azzurri* fared much better in their next two games, losing out narrowly to Argentina (25–16) and bowing out of the competition in fine style following an 18–15 win over Fiji. However, they still ended up on the bottom of their pool table.

They found themselves in a far tougher group four years later, alongside New Zealand, England and the United States. They won the match they realistically had to win against the United States in their tournament opener (30–9) and, although they lost out to both New Zealand (31–21) and England (36–6), their gritty performances in both games showed that Italian

rugby had come a long way.

It was much of the same in South Africa in 1995. Following the disappointment of an opening-game defeat to Western Samoa (42–18), they pushed England all the way in their second match, before losing out 27–20. But they carried their good form into their final game and came out on top of a high-scoring game against Argentina (31–25).

Italian rugby was starting to grow up. In 1997, they recorded two victories over Ireland and another win over France. The following year they added the scalp of Scotland to an ever-growing collection and, but for a questionable disallowed Alessandro Troncon try, might well have beaten England when the two met in a World Cup qualifier. As it was, England ran out 23–15 winners.

But it was an ageing Italian side that took to the field in the 1999 World Cup. They went home unhappy, losing heavily to England (67–7), narrowly to Tonga (28–25) and finding themselves on the wrong end of a 101–3 hammering at the hands of New Zealand.

In 2000, the Italians joined Europe's elite in the revamped and renamed Six Nations tournament. The timing could not have been worse. As shown by their performances in the 1999 World Cup, the players who had pushed Italy into the international rugby limelight were starting to come to the end of the road. They did win their first ever game 34–20 over Scotland in Rome, but it was Italy's lone victory in their first three Six Nations campaigns. However, when they beat Wales 30–22 in 2003, they avoided the wooden spoon for the first time and, given that the Welsh were in their pool for that year's World Cup, they could look forward to the tournament with some confidence.

It may have taken a slight knock when they lost their opening match against New Zealand 70–7, but subsequent victories over Tonga (36–12) and Canada (19–14) – the first time Italy had won two games at a World Cup – set up what was effectively a play-off with Wales for the group's last quarter-final spot. They lost, 27–15, and suffered World Cup disappointment once again. They were the only Six Nations team not to make it through to the last eight.

Italy struggled again in the 2004 Six Nations, although they did give their ever-growing support something to cheer about when they again beat Scotland 20–14 in Rome. However, their end-of-year report – with 42 points scored and 152 conceded – exposed their problems. So when they went winless the following year and picked up the wooden spoon yet again, it came as little surprise when the *Azzurri* and their New Zealand coach John Kirwan parted company. The Italian hierarchy turned to former France ace Pierre Berbizier as the man to arrest their slide down rugby's ladder.

And they made a decent fist of things in the 2006 Six Nations. They opened up with a competitive display against Ireland in Dublin, losing 26–16. They then led both France and England at half-time before running out of steam and losing to both. Then came an 18-all draw with Wales in Cardiff – a match that should have seen them end their tournament away duck – and they ended their campaign on the wrong side of a 13–10 scoreline against Scotland in Rome. They may have ended up on the bottom of the pile once again, but they had put in some commendable performances.

Under Berbizier, the *Azzurri* are starting to look a more disciplined and threatening unit. They beat Scotland at Murrayfield in the 2007 Six Nations – their first away victory in the competition – and will have to do so again if they want to take that great leap forward and reach the World Cup quarter-finals for the first time.

COACH
Pierre Berbizier
A former scrum-half and captain of the French side that dominated European rugby throughout the 1980s, Berbizier became coach of the France national side and led them to the semi-finals of the 1995 World Cup. He was sacked shortly afterwards and then became coach at Narbonne. He was appointed as Italian coach in 2006 and has been charged with bringing a more attacking style to Italian rugby.

 STAR PLAYER: Marco Bortolami

Position: Lock/captain
Born: 12 June 1980, Padova, Italy
Club: Gloucester
Height: 196cm **Weight:** 110kg
Caps: 54 **Points:** 30 (6t)
Debut: v. Namibia, 23 June 2001, Windhoek

The former Under-21 captain made his Italian debut as a 20-year-old against Namibia in 2001. Two years later he was appointed as his country's youngest ever captain when he led the *Azzurri* against the All Blacks. He picked up an injury in the opening match of the 2003 World Cup against Tonga and missed his country's crucial encounter with Wales – a match that saw Italy crash out of the tournament. Standout performances in the 2004 Six Nations tournament earned him a move to Narbonne. Following two successful seasons with the French club, he joined Gloucester in the summer of 2006 and stepped straight into the first team as captain.

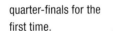

ROMANIA

PLAYING STRIP
Yellow shirts, blue shorts, red socks

FORM SINCE 2003 RUGBY WORLD CUP

Played:	29
Won:	18
Lost:	11
Drawn:	0
Winning percentage:	62.1%
Points for:	877
Points against:	598
Biggest victory:	97–0 v. Ukraine, 19 March 2005 at Bucharest
Heaviest defeat:	66–7 v. Wales, 12 November 2004 at Cardiff
Points scored per match:	30.2
Points conceded per match:	20.6

PAST WORLD CUP PERFORMANCES

1987	Group stages
1991	Group stages
1995	Group stages
1999	Group stages
2003	Group stages

COACH
Daniel Santamans

When Daniel Santamans was appointed as head coach of Romania in June 2004, he became the fourth Frenchman to lead the Oaks since the 2003 World Cup. He settled a wobbling Romanian ship, leading his charges to a shock 25–24 victory over Italy later that year and then saw Romania ease through the qualification process for the 2007 World Cup.

THE FALLEN OAKS

During the 1980s, there was a growing campaign for Romania to be added to the then Five Nations tournament, but the collapse of Communism and the advent of professionalism have seen the Oaks slide down world rugby's pecking order and the good times seem to be a thing of the past for Romanian rugby.

In many ways they were the pioneers of professional rugby. The governing Communist regime saw sport as a vital propaganda tool: funds were channelled directly to the national teams and the country's star players were employed by the army or the police and, in the case of rugby, they trained six days a week in the best facilities money could buy.

Romania started to emerge as a force on the world stage in the early 1980s. They had notched up some notable wins before but, after beating Wales 24–6 in 1983, they started to upset the formbook on a regular basis. Scotland's Grand Slam-winning team came to Bucharest in 1984 and lost. Romania travelled to the first World Cup full of confidence but – victory over Zimbabwe aside – they endured a disappointing tournament.

It was inevitable that Romanian rugby would suffer following the fall of Communism in 1989. Several leading players lost their lives during the revolution – including their captain Florica Murariu – and there would be no more handouts to the state-run teams.

But the national team continued to defy the odds. In 1990 they beat France on French soil (12–6). In 1991 they travelled to the World Cup in good heart, but a win in their final group game against Fiji (17–15) had been preceded by two defeats and they exited the tournament at the first hurdle. The pinch was starting to show in South Africa in 1995 when they crashed to three straight defeats and finished bottom of their pool.

The advent of professionalism hit Romanian rugby almost as hard as the revolution had done. As more than 200 players had to ply their trade overseas, the national team's form went into reverse. A solitary win over the United States was all they had to celebrate at the 1999 World Cup. And things didn't improve for them in 2003 either, with a final-game 37–7 victory over Namibia their only success. It's hard to see how things will improve for Romania in 2007.

STAR PLAYER: Ovidiu Tonita

Position: No.8/captain
Born: 26 August 1980, Barlad, Romania
Club: Perpignan (Fra)
Height: 195cm **Weight:** 105kg
Caps: 36 **Points:** 40 (8t)
Debut: v. Holland, 20 February 2000, Bucharest

The cornerstone of a powerful Romanian pack and a player who is not scared to mix it in every sense with the world's best players, Ovidiu Tonita made his debut against Holland in 2000 as a 20-year-old. He got his first taste of top-class rugby when he moved from Grenoble to Biarritz in 2002 and appeared in the Heineken Cup. Voted Romania's best player during the 2003 World Cup, the Herculean back-row forward secured a move to Perpignan in 2004 and has been an ever-present in the back row for the French club ever since. Renowned for his ferocity on the field of play, the Romanian captain is a player who leads from the front and is crucial to their World Cup hopes.

43

POOL C

LOS LOBOS *(The Wolves)*

PLAYING STRIP
Claret shirt with green trim, white shorts, green socks

FORM SINCE 2003 RUGBY WORLD CUP
Played:	32
Won:	18
Lost:	12
Drawn:	2
Winning percentage:	56.3%
Points for:	562
Points against:	674
Biggest victory:	52–14 v. Ukraine, 13 May 2006 at Lisbon
Heaviest defeat:	83–0 v. Italy, 7 October 2006 at L'Aquila
Points scored per match:	17.6
Points conceded per match:	21.1

PAST WORLD CUP PERFORMANCES
Debutants

COACH
Tomaz Morais
Coach of Portugal's Under-20, Under-21, sevens and 15-a-side teams, nobody has done more to shape a country's rugby fortunes than Tomaz Morais. Such was the respect he engendered he was nominated for the IRB Coach of the Year award in 2004, an unprecedented achievement for a coach from such a small rugby-playing nation. He may have lost out on that occasion, but secured the biggest prize of all when Portugal qualified for their first World Cup.

PORTUGAL

THE WOLVES FINALLY FIND THEIR BITE

A qualification process that started in November 2004 and which saw Portugal feature in 18 matches, finally saw the "Lobos" (the Wolves) secure a place in the World Cup for the first time. And in a country where football is the undisputed national pastime, it has taken a long time for rugby to enjoy the nation's sporting spotlight.

Portugal's first attempt at World Cup qualification in 1991 came to an abrupt halt following a defeat to Holland and they fell in the early qualifying phases for the second time in a row four years later. Matters improved in 1999. Having made it through to the latter qualifying stages for the first time, they found themselves in a play-off with Uruguay for a shootout for the final World Cup berth. The South Americans proved too strong for them and Portugal's rugby fortunes seemed to hit a new low when Spain ended their qualification chances in 2003.

But Portugal bounced back in style. They surprised everyone by taking the European Nations Cup in 2003–04 and entered the qualification process for the 2007 World Cup with justifiably high hopes. They made it through to the final qualification phase, a three-match series with Italy and Russia, with the winner gaining an automatic World Cup spot and the runner-up entering a series of repechage matches. An 83–0 opening loss to Italy may have been hard to stomach, but everyone knew that match had merely provided a predictable prelude to the group's main event: Portugal v. Russia in Lisbon with the winner facing Georgia in a winner-takes-all showdown. When it really mattered, Portugal won the day.

They may have suffered a 28–14 aggregate reverse to Georgia, but there was still cause for hope. When the Lobos edged out Morocco over two legs to set up a showdown with Uruguay for the final World Cup spot, Portugal's interest in the game hit an all-time high. A 3,000-strong capacity crowd cheered them to a 12–5 home victory and a nation erupted with joy when an 18–12 defeat in Montevideo secured a debut World Cup appearance courtesy of points difference. The cheers may well end there, but no one will want to deny Portugal their 240 minutes of rugby fame.

STAR PLAYER: DIOGO MATEUS

Position: *Inside-centre*
Born: *7 February 1980, Lisbon*
Club: *Munster (Ire)*
Height: *173cm* **Weight:** *80kg*
Caps: *30* **Points:** *24 (4t)*
Debut: *v. Georgia, 14 February 2004 in Tblisi*

Diogo Mateus became a national hero when he crashed over the line to secure a last-gasp 26–23 win over Russia that kept Portugal's hopes of qualifying for a first World Cup very much alive. It was significant perhaps that, in a side packed with amateurs, the hero was one of the few Portugal players with a pedigree in professional club rugby. Mateus rose through the ranks of club side Belenenses in his native Portugal, making his national debut on the wing in Portugal's away win over Georgia in 2004. He secured a dream move to Heineken Cup champions Munster in 2006.

PLAYING STRIP

Blue shirts with white piping, blue shorts, red socks

FORM SINCE 2003 RUGBY WORLD CUP

Played:	37
Won:	27
Lost:	9
Drawn:	1
Winning percentage:	73.0%
Points for:	1,072
Points against:	720
Biggest victory:	62–14 v. Romania, 17 June 2006 in Bucharest
Heaviest defeat:	47–3 v. New Zealand, 11 November 2006 in Lyon
Points scored per match:	29.0
Points conceded per match:	19.5

PAST WORLD CUP PERFORMANCES

1987	Runners-up
1991	Quarter-finals
1995	Semi-finals
1999	Runners-up
2003	Semi-finals

Fabien Pelous: Another player who missed the 2007 Six Nations Championship, the Toulouse lock looks set to become France's most capped player during the 2007 World Cup.

FRANCE

DESPERATE FOR WORLD CUP GLORY

The tournament hosts will be desperate to emulate their football peers and lift the World Cup for the first time on home soil. But despite a successful 2007 Six Nations campaign, the jury is still out on Bernard Laporte's France. Do they have what it takes to become the world champions?

It certainly looked as though they did in 1987 when they travelled to Australia and New Zealand for the inaugural World Cup. Off the back of a Five Nations Grand Slam, they got off to an inauspicious start with a 20–20 draw against Scotland in their opening game. The failure to win seemed to kick-start their campaign. Comfortable victories over Romania (55–12) and Zimbabwe (70–12) followed and France topped their group on points difference.

They faced Fiji in the quarter-finals and romped to a 31–16 victory to book their place in the semi-finals against co-hosts Australia. It was a game the Wallabies, the pre-tournament favourites, were expected to win. France had other ideas and, in what is widely considered the best game ever played in a World Cup, they stunned Australia in the final moments of the game with a Serge Blanco try to steal a famous 30–24 victory.

But as hot as French rugby can blow, it can also be just as cold, and it was a distinctly chilly France that turned out against New Zealand at Eden Park in the final. From the moment All Black winger John Kirwan crossed the line to score New Zealand's opening try, there was only going to be one winner. France lost 29–9 and were left to lick their wounds.

They finished on top of their group four years later when the tournament came to the northern hemisphere, but their performances, particularly the manner of their 19–13 struggle to victory over Canada, left many questioning France's World Cup credentials. England, the reigning Five Nations champions, would present an altogether stiffer challenge in the last eight. Too stiff as it turned out: a dogged England ran out 19–10 winners in Paris.

Opening victories over the Ivory Coast and Tonga in 1995 set up a clash for top spot in the pool against Scotland, and although France scraped through the match 22–19, they hardly seemed to be playing at the top of their game. A 36–12 win over Ireland in the quarter-finals seemed to indicate they were back on track, but they were stymied by the weather when they faced hosts South Africa in the first of the semi-finals in Durban. Heavy pre-match rain had left the King's Park pitch waterlogged – hardly the ideal platform for France's attacking brand of rugby – and Les Bleus were edged out 19–15.

France went into the 1999 World Cup on the back of a desperately disappointing Five Nations campaign – one that had seen them finish bottom – but three straight victories, admittedly against comparatively weak opposition, saw them finish on top of their group. They faced Argentina in the quarter-finals and eased to a 47–26 victory. Nobody gave them a chance in the semi-finals against New Zealand. But, as we have seen already, when France blow hot they can play some scintillating rugby. They produced one of the greatest second-half performances in the history of the game to stun the All Blacks 43–31. How the French must have wished the tournament could have ended there. They disappointed once again in the final and Australia were able to cruise to a 35–12 win.

And they weren't among the favourites in 2003 either, but still managed to cruise unbeaten through their pool to face Ireland in the quarter-finals. The Irish were no match

for them and, following a 43–21 victory, France cantered to a semi-final showdown against England. And that's where French hopes came to an end. On a rainy night in Sydney, France found themselves on the receiving end of a Jonny Wilkinson kicking lesson and went down to a 24–7 defeat.

A 24–21 victory over England in the final game of the 2004 Six Nations to secure the Grand Slam eased a little of their World Cup pain. And a 27–14 autumn win over Australia added a spring to their step. They looked set to defend their Six Nations crown in 2005, until Wales came to town and ran out 24–18 winners – en route to their first Grand Slam for 28 years – and France had to settle for the runners-up spot. They went one better in 2006. After suffering the shock of an opening defeat to Scotland at Murrayfield, they rallied to win their final four games to collect the Six Nations title.

And victory over South Africa in Cape Town in the summer of 2006 seemed to confirm that French rugby was firmly back on the right track. New Zealand then derailed their momentum as France capitulated to two hapless defeats in the space of seven days.

But they seemed to be returning to something like their best form during the 2007 Six Nations Championship, easing their way to the title. England went into the last World Cup on the back of winning the Six Nations and emerged as world champions. The whole of France is hoping that history repeats itself.

COACH
Bernard Laporte
With a face that has become synonymous with French rugby, Bernard Laporte became the first fully professional head coach of France in 1999. Before that he made his name with Stade Français. Joining them in 1995 he steered them from the third division to champions in four seasons. Under his direction France won Six Nations titles in 2002, 2004 (achieving the Grand Slam) and 2006. He will leave the post following the 2007 World Cup. French rugby will miss him.

 STAR PLAYER: Yannick Jauzion

Position: Centre
Born: 28 July 1978, Castres, France
Club: Toulouse
Height: 193cm **Weight:** 101kg
Debut: 11 November 2003 v. Ireland at Melbourne
Caps: 42 **Points:** 73 (14t, 1dg)

Yannick Jauzion is the complete rugby player. Tall, strong, pacy and with an eye for the smallest of gaps, he has firmly established himself as one of the game's greatest attacking threats. The centre was a pivotal member of the Toulouse side that reached the Heineken Cup final for three years in a row (2003–05) and made his debut for France in a quarter-final victory over Ireland in the 2003 World Cup. Jauzion's first international try came against the same opponents, a few months later, on his Six Nations debut. Injury saw him miss out on the 2006 Six Nations but, restored to full fitness, he has become one of the first names on Bernard Laporte's teamsheet as France build towards World Cup glory.

IRELAND

PLAYING STRIP

Green shirts with white trim, white shorts, green socks

FORM SINCE 2003 RUGBY WORLD CUP

Played:	36
Won:	24
Lost:	12
Drawn:	0
Winning percentage:	66.7%
Points for:	985
Points against:	711
Biggest victory:	61–17 v. Pacific Islanders, 26 November 2006 in Dublin
Heaviest defeat:	45–7 v. New Zealand, 12 November 2005 in Dublin
Points scored per match:	27.4
Points conceded per match:	19.7

PAST WORLD CUP PERFORMANCES

1987	Quarter-finals
1991	Quarter-finals
1995	Quarter-finals
1999	Quarter-final play-offs
2003	Quarter-finals

BURSTING WITH TALENT

This talented generation of Irish players is now at its peak. They have enjoyed recent success over their Six Nations counterparts and have recorded wins over every southern hemisphere opponent bar New Zealand. There's a sense of now or never for this particular group of Ireland players.

Such a period of success is uncharted territory for Ireland. Their first appearance in the World Cup coincided with a relative slump in Irish rugby fortunes, and although nobody really expected them to challenge for the top honours, they would have been disappointed to fall to Wales 13–6 in their opening game. They rallied to secure comfortable victories over Canada and Tonga, but the defeat to the Welsh condemned them to second place in the pool and a tough quarter-final tie against pre-tournament favourites Australia. The step up in class was too much: Ireland crashed to a 33–15 defeat and a premature exit.

A disappointing 24–15 defeat to Scotland in Ireland's final pool game in 1991 meant second place in the pool once again and the prospect of another quarter-final match-up against the Wallabies. This time they fared much better. With the game entering its final moments,

Ireland held a slender lead and the Lansdowne Road crowd were starting to sense a shock victory. But Michael Lynagh slipped over the line at the death to steal a 19–18 victory. They Irish were heartbroken, and rightly so: they have not come as close to reaching the semi-finals of the World Cup since.

France proved Ireland's quarter-final nemesis when the tournament arrived in South Africa four years later, but in many respects the Irish would have been happy to have got there in the first place. Drawn in a tough group alongside New Zealand, Wales and Japan, they recovered from an opening 43–19 reverse against the All Blacks to beat Japan 50–28. That left an enthralling showdown with Wales in what was effectively a play-off for second place in the group and a place in the quarter-finals. In a nervy encounter, the Irish came out on top by the narrowest of margins (24–23) to earn their shot

Paul O'Connell: A string of stand-out performances have earned the Munster lock a glittering reputation. If Ireland are to achieve World Cup glory, he will have to be at his very best.

against the French. They lost 36–12, but at least their World Cup standards weren't slipping.

They did four years later. Second place in the group behind Australia meant a play-off against Argentina for the right to play France in the quarter-finals. Argentina won the day and Ireland departed the tournament with plenty to think about.

It marked a turning point in Irish rugby. Although Ireland's provincial sides had been turned into de facto club sides following the advent of professionalism in 1995, it wasn't until the foundation of the Celtic League in 2001 that Irish professionals – for so long forced overseas in their quest for top-class rugby – returned to the Emerald Isle in their droves, satisfied that, at last, their homeland could satisfy their need for competitive rugby. International players played with and against each other on a regular basis and strong bonds started to form. The main beneficiary was the Ireland national team.

The results started to show. They finished second in the 2001 Six Nations tournament and then went on a ten-match unbeaten run into 2003, including four straight matches in the Six Nations. But England brought the record to a dramatic end, dominating the Grand Slam decider at Lansdowne Road and running out comfortable 42–6 winners, but at least Ireland travelled to the World Cup seven months later in good shape.

And how well they played, opening with three straight wins to set up a final-match showdown for the pool's top spot against Australia. They pushed the hosts all the way, but again lost by a single point, 17–16. It was a costly defeat: it condemned the Irish to a quarter-final against the French, who strolled to a comfortable 43–21 victory.

They finished as second best to Les Bleus in the following year's Six Nations, settling for the runners-up spot but surely having taken huge satisfaction from becoming the first side to beat England since their World Cup success. Ireland entered the following year's tournament as slight favourites and, after winning their opening three games and starting to dream of a first Grand Slam since 1948, lost 26–19 to France at Lansdowne Road. A defeat to Wales to round off their campaign left them in third place and bitterly disappointed.

They picked up their second Triple Crown in three years in 2006, but once again the French dashed any dreams of a Grand Slam with a comfortable 43–31 win in Paris. Good performances in defeat against New Zealand followed, before Australia and South Africa were well beaten at Lansdowne Road in the 2006 autumn series of Tests.

A poor 20 minutes against France aside, Ireland played some great rugby during the 2007 Six Nations Championship, including a record victory over England at Croke Park and another Triple Crown. However, question marks remain as to whether Ireland have the forward muscle to win the game's greatest prize.

COACH
Eddie O'Sullivan

Eddie O'Sullivan's appointment as national coach changed the fortunes of Irish rugby. They embarked on a record-breaking ten-match unbeaten run before losing at home to England in March 2003. There have been other highlights as well: he led Ireland to their first Triple Crown in 19 years and in 2004 masterminded his side's first win over South Africa since 1965.

STAR PLAYER: Brian O'Driscoll

Position: Centre
Born: 21 January 1979, Dublin, Ireland
Club: Leinster
Height: 180cm **Weight:** 95kg
Caps: 74 **Points:** 157 (29t, 4dg)
Debut: v. Australia, 12 June 1999, Ballymore

Picked for Ireland's summer tour to Australia in 1999, O'Driscoll quickly established himself as a world-class centre and it wasn't long before he had become a permanent fixture in the Ireland back-line. He starred on the British Lions tour to Australia in 2001, playing in all three Tests. Then, in 2003, following the retirement of Keith Wood, he was awarded the captaincy of Ireland. He led them to second place in the Six Nations and the Triple Crown. He then led the British Lions to New Zealand, but his tour ended in the opening moments of the first Test when a controversial tackle resulted in a dislocated shoulder. He returned to action in December 2005, leading Ireland to another Triple Crown and being voted the 2006 Six Nations player of the tournament.

PLAYING STRIP

Light blue and white hooped shirts, white shorts, light blue and white socks

FORM SINCE 2003 RUGBY WORLD CUP

Played:	27
Won:	16
Lost:	10
Drawn:	1
Winning percentage:	59.3%
Points for:	943
Points against:	655
Biggest victory:	147–7 v. Venezuela, 1 May 2004 in Santiago
Heaviest defeat:	41–7 v. New Zealand, 26 June 2004 in Hamilton
Points scored per match:	34.9
Points conceded per match:	24.3

PAST WORLD CUP PERFORMANCES

1987	Group stages
1991	Group stages
1995	Group stages
1999	Quarter-finals
2003	Group stages

Augustin Pichot: The veteran scrum-half, now plying his trade with French club Stade Français, forms a vital half-back partnership with the electric Felipe Contepomi.

ARGENTINA

POWERFUL PUMAS

Argentina are the only top-ranked nation in world rugby not to play in a regular competition, but that has not stopped them from providing a major challenge to their opponents. Participants in every World Cup to date, they could well be the shock team of the tournament.

By the time they took their place in the inaugural World Cup in 1987, Argentina had already formed a fearsome reputation. They were almost invincible at home, had recorded wins over England, France and Australia, drawn with New Zealand and would have had their eyes firmly set on a place in the quarter-finals.

A shock 28–9 loss to Fiji in their opening game put them firmly on the back foot. Victory over Italy in their next match meant that they would have to pull off the greatest upset in their history and beat New Zealand if they wanted to stay in the competition. The All Blacks cruised to a 46–15 victory and Argentina's interest in the competition was over.

It was a body blow for Argentine rugby. A number of their senior players called it a day and it was a new-look Puma side that took to the field at the 1991 World Cup. They were disappointing, losing all three of their matches to finish on the bottom of their pool.

By the time Argentina exited the tournament in South Africa in 1995, the world's rugby media were hailing the Pumas' pack as the most fearsome eight in the world. It had caused major problems for England, Western Samoa and Italy. The only problem was that Argentina could not capitalize on their forward dominance and ended up losing all three of their pool games for the second World Cup in a row.

But it was an altogether more experienced side that travelled to the northern hemisphere four years later. They shrugged off the disappointment of an opening 23–18 defeat to Wales to beat Western Samoa (32–16) and Japan (33–12) to earn a place in a play-off against Ireland for a shot at a place in the last eight. And in front of a disbelieving Lansdowne Road

crowd, the Pumas held their nerve to emerge 28–24 winners. Their reward was a quarter-final showdown against France in Paris. But following a 47–26 defeat, that is where their interest in the tournament ended. It remains their best World Cup performance to date.

They opened their 2003 campaign with a 24–8 defeat to hosts Australia. Comfortable victories over Namibia and Romania followed to set up a clash with Ireland at the Adelaide Oval. If the Pumas could repeat the result of four years earlier they would reach the last eight for the second successive tournament. But it was the Irish who held their nerve this time to emerge 16–15 winners. Disappointed they may have been, but the Pumas were now starting to challenge the elite of world rugby, both at home and away, on a regular basis.

The Pumas' remained dominant over their South American neighbours in 2004, but it was the series of matches that followed that showed just how far their game was developing. Wales, who would go on to complete a Six Nations Grand Slam the following year, came to Argentina and could only draw a two-match series. The Pumas then travelled to New Zealand and suffered a 41–7 defeat. Then came a trip to France: Argentina recorded one of their best results for years to shock the French 24–14. A week later they travelled to Dublin to face Ireland and pushed them all the way, only to lose out 21–19. They ended the year with a 39–7 home defeat at the hands South Africa.

Argentina, boasting mostly second- and third-choice players, provided the opposition for the 2005 British Lions' final warm-up game before their tour to New Zealand. They almost provided an upset, with only Jonny Wilkinson's injury-time penalty saving the Lions' blushes to salvage a 25–25 draw. Back to full strength later in the year, they beat Scotland at Murrayfield – the fifth consecutive time they had beaten the Scots since 1990 – and added another Six Nations scalp with a 39–22 defeat of Italy in Genoa.

They took that form into 2006, notching up a series win over a second-string Wales side and pushing the All Blacks all the way in Buenos Aires, only to fall 25–19. And the autumn series of Tests in Europe later in the year showed just how far the Pumas had come. Victory over England at Twickenham (25–18) saw them leapfrog the world champions in the world rankings. They then beat Italy 23–16 and, a week later, their forwards shone once more in a narrow 27–26 defeat to France.

Amid growing clamours for Argentina to be admitted to an expanded Six Nations tournament, the Pumas are developing into one of the giants of the world game. If you are looking for a team to provide an upset at the 2007 World Cup then look no further than the men in white and blue. Given their performances in recent times, a victory over France or Ireland might not come as such a shock at all.

PLAYERS TO WATCH

Miguel Avramovic
Age 26 Position Centre
Club Worcester Caps 5
Points 15 (3t)

Omar Hasan
Age 36 Position Prop
Club Toulouse (Fra) Caps 57
Points 15 (3t)

Juan Martin Fernandez Lobbe
Age 26 Position Back row
Club Sale Sharks Caps 9
Points 15 (3t)

Agustin Pichot
Age 33 Position Scrum-half/captain
Club Stade Français Caps 65
Points 60 (12t)

Federico Todeschini
Age 32 Position Fly-half/full-back
Club Béziers (Fra) Caps 6
Points 167 (1t, 27c, 36p)

COACH
Marcelo Loffreda
Having made 44 appearances for the Pumas at centre, one of them as captain, Marcelo Loffreda retired from playing in 1994 to become a coach. Six years later he was placed in charge of the national side. The association has been a happy one. Argentina have secured series wins over England, France, Wales and Scotland under his command.

★ STAR PLAYER: Felipe Contepomi

Position: Fly-half
Born: 20 August 1977, Buenos Aires, Argentina
Club: Leinster
Height: 180cm **Weight:** 93kg
Caps: 48 **Points:** 307 (7t, 40c, 63p, 1dg)
Debut: v. Chile, 10 October 1998

It's no easy thing wearing the No.10 shirt in Argentina – it will forever be associated with footballer Diego Maradona – but few have worn it with as much panache as Felipe Contepomi. A veteran of two World Cups, he is compared favourably in some quarters to New Zealand's Dan Carter. Growing up in a strong rugby family in Buenos Aires, he first came to Europe to play for Bristol in 2003. Then, in 2004, he secured a lucrative move to Leinster. He took Irish rugby by storm, breaking the scoring record in the Celtic League and winning legions of fans with his attacking style of play. And his blossoming half-back partnership with Augustin Pichot has been instrumental in the Pumas' recent rise up the world rankings.

GEORGIA

POOL D
LELOS

PLAYING STRIP
Black shirts with burgundy trim, black
shorts, black socks

FORM SINCE 2003 RUGBY WORLD CUP
Played:	25
Won:	14
Lost:	9
Drawn:	2
Winning percentage:	56.0%
Points for:	602
Points against:	372
Biggest victory:	75–10 v. Czech Republic,
	12 June 2005 at Kutaisi
Heaviest defeat:	35–10 v. Romania,
	25 February 2006 at Bucharest
Points scored per match:	24.1
Points conceded per match:	14.9

PAST WORLD CUP PERFORMANCES
1987	Did not enter
1991	Did not enter
1995	Failed to qualify
1999	Failed to qualify
2003	Group stages

COACH
Malkhaz Cheishvili
A former scrum-half who played four times
for Georgia between 1989 and 1995, Malkhaz Cheishvili, who had been the long-term
coach of the national Sevens team, took
charge of the national team following the
departure of Claude Saurel from the post.

SLOWLY MAKING THEIR MARK
For a side with few resources – they had to use old Soviet tractors for scrum
machines – even getting to the World Cup represents a huge achievement for
Georgia and they will be out to enjoy themselves in their second successive
tournament appearance.

Although rugby has been played in Georgia since the
1920s, their best players were forced to play for the
Soviet Union. Things started to change in April 1991
when Georgia gained its independence and a year later
the country was admitted to the International Rugby
Board and could play regular internationals as a country
in its own right.

They almost made it to the 1999 World Cup, falling
to Romania over a two-legged play-off on points
difference. Then Frenchman Claude Saurel took charge.
He led them to second place in the European Nations
Cup in 2000, losing out narrowly to Romania once
again. They shocked the Oaks in Bucharest a year
later, winning the final match of the European Nations
Cup 31–20 to collect their first major prize. When they
finished a respectable tenth in the 2001 Sevens World
Cup, interest in the game started to explode. Russia
came to town in 2002 and 65,000 crammed into the
national stadium in Tblisi to witness the 12–12 draw.

A year later the two countries faced off at the same
venue: this time a place in the 2003 World Cup finals
was at stake. Cheered on by a vociferous crowd, Georgia
hung on to a famous 17–14 victory. A country danced in
the streets.

They may have lost all four games in Australia –
including a disappointing 24–12 defeat to Uruguay – but
the Georgians would have loved every minute of their
first taste of the game's greatest tournament. And from
the moment they left the shores of Australia their No. 1
priority was to make sure they qualified for France 2007.

And when they overcame Portugal in a two-legged
play-off (winning 17–3 in Tblisi and drawing 11–11 in
Lisbon) it was mission accomplished. Although a victory
against the big boys in their group will almost certainly
be beyond them, there is every chance that they can
overcome Namibia in Lens on 26 September to record
their first ever World Cup victory. And how a nation
would cheer.

STAR PLAYER: Paliko Jimsheladze

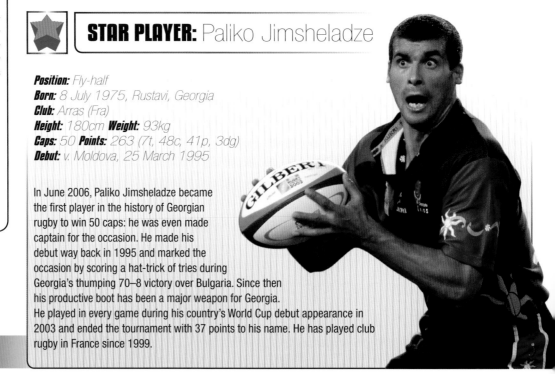

Position: Fly-half
Born: 8 July 1975, Rustavi, Georgia
Club: Arras (Fra)
Height: 180cm *Weight:* 93kg
Caps: 50 *Points:* 263 (7t, 48c, 41p, 3dg)
Debut: v. Moldova, 25 March 1995

In June 2006, Paliko Jimsheladze became
the first player in the history of Georgian
rugby to win 50 caps: he was even made
captain for the occasion. He made his
debut way back in 1995 and marked the
occasion by scoring a hat-trick of tries during
Georgia's thumping 70–8 victory over Bulgaria. Since then
his productive boot has been a major weapon for Georgia.
He played in every game during his country's World Cup debut appearance in
2003 and ended the tournament with 37 points to his name. He has played club
rugby in France since 1999.

NAMIBIA

PLAYING STRIP

Blue shirt with white, red and yellow trim, blue shorts, black socks

FORM SINCE 2003 RUGBY WORLD CUP

Played:	14
Won:	10
Lost:	4
Drawn:	0
Winning percentage:	71.4%
Points for:	529
Points against:	239
Biggest victory:	84–12 v. Kenya, 27 May 2006 at Windhoek
Heaviest defeat:	49–0 v. Morocco, 5 November 2005 at Casablanca
Points scored per match:	37.8
Points conceded per match:	17.1

PAST WORLD CUP PERFORMANCES

1987	Did not enter
1991	Did not enter
1995	Did not qualify
1999	Group stages
2003	Group stages

COACH
Johannes Venter

Venter, who took charge following the acrimonious departure of previous coach Dave Waterston, was the toast of Namibia after he guided his side through what turned out to be a tough campaign to qualify for their third consecutive World Cup finals. However, he will be more than aware that tougher challenges lie ahead for his side in France.

ANY VICTORY WILL DO

Since gaining independence from South Africa in 1990, Namibia have gone on to appear in the World Cup in both 1999 and 2003; but that is where the good news ends. They may have become serial qualifiers for the tournament, but they are still waiting for a victory on the world's biggest stage.

Prior to gaining their independence from South Africa, Namibia appeared in the Currie Cup as South West Africa and achieved a best finish of third in 1989. And they took to international rugby in 1991 like ducks to water, notching up impressive series wins over both Ireland and Italy on their way to a ten-match unbeaten start in international rugby.

Their first real test came when they tried to secure qualification for the 1995 World Cup, and the fact that it would be hosted by South Africa, their colonial fathers, gave added motivation. However, a defeat to the Ivory Coast and a draw with Morocco left their World Cup dreams in tatters.

They gained revenge in the qualification process for the 1999 World Cup to take their place among world rugby's elite for the first time, but their first taste of rugby's biggest tournament turned out to be a miserable experience. Their record of played three, lost three, did not make for happy reading and

only Italy conceded more points in the tournament. However, they would have taken great heart from their performance against France, where they took an early lead and held the French for the first 20 minutes before slipping to a 35–13 defeat.

Having secured qualification for the 2003 tournament they fared no better, and when they found themselves on the back end of a 142–0 drubbing to Australia, it sparked a vociferous debate about whether or not rugby minnows such as Namibia should play in the World Cup. For the record, Namibia conceded a massive 310 points in the 2003 World Cup and scored a paltry 28.

Qualification for the 2007 tournament did not come easily. Shock defeats to Kenya and Tunisia left them facing a play-off against Morocco. They won both legs convincingly. They will be hoping it is third time lucky in France 2007 and their game against Georgia could well see them record their first ever World Cup victory.

 STAR PLAYER: KEES LENSING

Position: Prop/captain
Born: 1 June 1978
Club: Natal Sharks
Height: 190cm *Weight:* 122kg
Caps: 10 *Points:* 5 (1t)
Debut: v. Madagascar, 15 June 2002, Windhoek, Namibia

One of the strongest props in world rugby, Kees Lensing is a highly effective and powerful scrummager who made his debut for Namibia in his side's open qualifying game for the 2003 World Cup against Madagascar. He has been one of the first names on the Namibian teamsheet ever since. He has also had an impressive club career in both the northern and southern hemispheres. After three years with the Bulls, he turned his back on Super 12 rugby in the autumn of 2005 to play for the Leeds Tykes, but returned to the renamed Super 14 with the Natal Sharks in 2007.

Welcome to La Belle France

From high-mountain Alpine ranges to lush, verdant countryside, from chic city boulevards catering for the eager *fashionistas'* every need to mile upon mile of rich agricultural terrain and from pulsing industrial heartlands to the tranquillity of a traditional hilltop town, France is a compellingly subtle blend; a mix of old and new, a fusion of both northern and southern Europe. Renowned for food that can satisfy even the most reluctant taste buds, wine that can tantalize the palates of even the savviest wine buffs and an array of cheeses that can leave even the most sophisticated diners bewildered, France has justifiably earned the reputation as being the gastronomical centre of the world. And the French themselves are proud of those claims: they believe their way of life to be unbeatable. Spend some time there and you'll find it hard to disagree.

FRENCH RUGBY TOP TENS

MOST POINTS

Name	Career	Points
Christophe Lamaison	1996–2001	380
Thierry Lacroix	1989–97	367
Didier Camberabero	1982–91	354
Gérald Merceron	1999–2003	267
Jean-Pierre Romeu	1972–77	265
Thomas Castaignède	1995–present	252
Frédéric Michalak	2001–06	243
Serge Blanco	1980–91	233
Dimitri Yachvili	2002–present	220
Jean-Patrick Lescarboura	1982–90	196

MOST CAPS

Name	Career	Caps
Philippe Sella	1982–95	111
Fabien Pelous	1995–present	110
Serge Blanco	1980–91	93
Raphael Ibanez	1996–present	88
Olivier Magne	1997–present	88
Abdelatif Benazzi	1990–2001	78
Olivier Brouzet	1994–2003	71
Jean-Luc Sadourny	1991–2001	71
Christian Califano	1994–2001	70
Roland Bertranne	1971–81	69

MOST TRIES

Name	Career	Tries
Serge Blanco	1980–91	38
Philippe Saint-André	1990–97	32
Philippe Sella	1982–95	31
Philippe Bernat-Salles	1992–2001	26
Emile Ntamack	1994–2000	26
Christian Darrouy	1957–67	23
Christophe Dominici	1998–present	23
Patrice Lagisquet	1983–91	20
Jean Dupuy	1956–64	19
Aurélien Rougerie	2001–present	19

FROM HUMBLE BEGINNINGS TO KINGS OF EUROPE

Given France's proximity to England, it was only a matter of time before rugby travelled across the Channel. It finally arrived on French soil in 1872, but it took some time before France emerged as a true force on the world rugby scene and their journey to the top of the game has been anything but smooth.

By 1910 France had been admitted to the Five Nations' fold, but sporadic victories over Scotland and Ireland aside, they hardly set the competition on fire. They had to wait until 1927 before they recorded a win over England and the following year before they did the same to Wales. And just when it seemed as though French rugby was on the up, France made the headlines for all the wrong reasons: their ferocious style of play had been upsetting their Five Nations opponents for some time, but when rumours of professionalism in French rugby started to emerge in 1932, France were duly banished from the tournament. Condemned to playing matches against the likes of Germany, Italy and Romania, France went on a winning streak, notching ten consecutive wins between 1931 and 1936; it remains a national record, but France yearned for a return to more competitive rugby.

The Second World War put paid to any of hopes of that, and it wasn't until peace had resumed in Europe and rugby returned to the international sporting calendar in 1947 that France were reinstated into Europe's premier rugby competition. They seemed like a different side.

It took some time, but results started to improve. In 1954 they beat the All Blacks for the first time, 3–0 at the Stade Colombes in Paris. In 1958, France travelled to South Africa for a two-Test series as massive underdogs. They surprised everybody by hanging on for a 3–3 draw in the first Test at Newlands, Cape Town. But if that was a shock, their 9–5 victory at Ellis Park, Johannesburg, a week later sent tremors around the rugby world. French rugby had finally come of age: they were now part of the sport's elite.

They continued in the Five Nations where they had left off in South Africa, claiming the championship for the first time outright in 1959 and did not relinquish the trophy for the next four years. In the late 1960s and early '70s they became one of the pre-eminent sides in Europe, winning the Grand Slam for the first time in 1968 and, with Jo Maso, Pierre Villepreux and co. in harness, went toe to toe with the great Welsh sides of the era, winning the tournament in 1967, following it up with a Grand Slam the following year and sharing top spot in both 1970 and 1973. They romped to Grand Slam glory once again in 1977 and, when they beat the All Blacks 24–19 on 14 July 1979, Bastille Day celebrations back in France were all the sweeter.

When former scrum-half Jacques Fouroux took over as coach in 1980 it signalled the start of an unprecedented period of success for French rugby. Led by their talismanic shock-haired skipper Jean-Pierre

At last: France, having shared the 1965 Five Nations championship, and won it outright in 1966 and 1967, finally claimed their first Grand Slam with a victory in Cardiff in March 1968.

Cream of the continent: Les Bleus conquered all before them in 2004 to record their sixth Grand Slam. By recording further Six Nations championship successes in both 2006 and 2007, the French could rightly lay claim to the title of "The Rugby Kings of Europe".

Rives, and with the dazzling talents of Serge Blanco and Philippe Sella in the backs, they won six Five Nations titles and two Grand Slams in a decade.

They travelled to the inaugural World Cup in 1987 on the back of the second of those Grand Slams, but nobody expected them to beat favourites Australia in the semi-finals. It turned out to be the greatest game ever played in the history of the World Cup. With seconds remaining on the clock, Serge Blanco squeezed over the line to secure a 30–24 victory. If only they could have repeated that form in the final: as if exhausted by their semi-final success, France barely turned up and New Zealand won 29–9.

It was as close as they have come to lifting the game's most prestigious trophy. When they suffered an embarrassing 12–6 loss to Romania on home soil a year later, Fouroux was given the sack. They entered the 1991 World Cup out of form and suffered a quarter-final exit at the hands of England – their worst showing in a World Cup to date. But it was a different France that

turned up in South Africa in 1995. They marched through the tournament to reach the semi-finals, but fell to hosts South Africa on a waterlogged pitch in Durban.

Back-to-back victories in the Five Nations in 1997 and 1998 meant they would have entered the 1999 World Cup in good heart. And how well they played, finishing on top of their group and brushing aside the attentions of Argentina in the quarter-finals to face a semi-final showdown against New Zealand. Just as had been the case in 1987, it was a last-four clash nobody expected France to win. And just as had been the case 12 years earlier, France, playing some of the most delightful attacking rugby ever seen, shocked the pre-tournament favourites to run out 43–31 winners. However, once again they had reserved their best performance for the semi-finals, and Australia cruised to their second world crown in the final at the Millennium Stadium following a comfortable 35–12 victory.

They may have collected a Grand Slam in the new Six Nations tournament in 2002, but nobody really rated their chances to collect the world crown. And they suffered semi-final anguish once again as the metronomic boot of England's Jonny Wilkinson dashed their World Cup dreams. However, they have continued to enjoy success in Europe, picking up the title in 2004 (with a Grand Slam), 2006 and 2007, and by the time they host the 2007 World Cup, only New Zealand will lie ahead of them in the world rankings.

FIVE OF THE BEST

THE ALL-TIME GREATS OF FRENCH RUGBY

Rugby is anything but a one-dimensional game: the beauty of flowing back play is matched by the dynamic muscularity of forwards standing toe-to-toe, unflinching, refusing to give an inch. To see rugby at its best is to see the ball passed rapidly through the hands; it is to see backs darting through the slightest of gaps, leaving defenders trailing in their wake. It is to see the fearsome all-action tackle that stops an attacker in his tracks or the shuddering power of a scrum. These are the characteristics that define French rugby: fast, open and attacking.

↑ JEAN PRAT

Born: 1 August 1923, Lourdes, France
Position: Flanker
Caps: 51
Points: 145 (9t, 26c, 15p, 5dg)
Debut: 1 January 1945 v. British Army at Paris
Last game: 10 April 1955 v. Italy at Grenoble

A pioneer of total rugby, Jean Prat was one of the prime architects of France's post-war rise into world rugby's elite following their exclusion from top-class European rugby in 1931. He was part of the 1948 side that won for the first time on Welsh soil, but it was his performance against England in 1951 that earned him the moniker "Monsieur Rugby" – he scored a try, a conversion and a drop-goal. Awarded the captaincy in 1953, he scored the only try in France's historic 3–0 victory over the 1954 All Blacks and led his side to a share of the Five Nations crown the same year: both being French firsts. He transferred his leadership skills to coaching the national side and cemented his place further in the pantheon of French rugby history when he led them to their first Grand Slam, in 1968, his final year in charge. He died in February 2005.

↓ JO MASO

Born: 27 December 1944, Toulouse, France
Position: Centre
Caps: 25
Points: 16 (4t)
Debut: 9 April 1966 v. Italy at Naples
Last game: 11 November 1973 v. Romania at Agen

A speedy and elusive runner, Jo Maso embodied the style and panache that have become hallmarks of French rugby. He made his debut against Italy in 1966 and was an integral part of the 1968 side that showed the world just how far French rugby had come. Having beaten Ireland, England and Scotland all that stood between France and a first Grand Slam were Wales at Cardiff Arms' Park. A rain-soaked pitch prevented the French from producing the free-flowing running rugby for which they were becoming famous, but their hard-fought triumph was cause enough for French celebrations. Maso remained an important part of the French set-up after his retirement in 1973. He was part of the management trio – alongside Jean-Claude Skrela and Pierre Villepreux – that guided France to back-to-back Grand Slams in 1997 and 1998 and to the World Cup final in 1999 and remains an integral part of the French management set-up to this day.

↘ SERGE BLANCO

Born: 31 August 1958, Caracas, Venezuela
Position: Full-back/wing
Caps: 93
Points: 233 (38t, 6c, 21p, 2dg)
Debut: 8 November 1980 v. South Africa at Cape Town
Last game: 19 October 1991 v. England at Paris

← JEAN-PIERRE RIVES

Born: 31 December 1952, Toulouse, France
Position: Flanker
Caps: 59
Points: 20 (5t)
Debut: 1 February 1975 v. England at Twickenham
Last game: 17 March 1984 v. Scotland at Murrayfield

Jean-Pierre Rives was the first true celebrity of French rugby. He made his debut in France's 27–20 win over England in 1975 and formed an immediate rapport with Jean-Claude Skrela; the back-row pair formed a formidable partnership that helped sweep France to two memorable Grand Slams in 1977 and 1981 (the latter with Rives as captain). This was the time when France would run the ball from anywhere on the field, but such champagne rugby was only possible because of Rives's exceptional recycling abilities: he was a textbook tackler, had exemplary handling skills and an uncanny ability to keep the ball alive. He captained France to a first win over the All Blacks in New Zealand and to further Five Nations success in 1983 (shared with Ireland). He retired in 1984 and has gone on to become a highly regarded sculptor. He played an influential role in France's bid to host the 2007 World Cup.

When he retired Serge Blanco had 93 caps and 38 tries to his name, despite famously smoking 60 cigarettes a day. Born in Caracas, Venezuela, he grew up in France and made his debut for Biarritz in 1975. Five years later he made his debut on the wing against South Africa. His first international try came in France's opening 1981 Five Nations match against Scotland. France went on to win the Grand Slam. There was no greater sight than to see him running with ball in hand and he had an uncanny ability to swing a match in his team's favour. There is no finer example than the dramatic try he scored in the 1987 World Cup semi-final against Australia where his moment of last-minute, brilliant individualism took his side through to the final. Awarded the captaincy in 1990, he retired a year later following France's World Cup quarter-final defeat to England.

← PHILIPPE SELLA

Born: 14 February 1962, Tonneins, France
Position: Centre
Caps: 111
Points: 125 (30t)
Debut: 31 October 1982 v. Romania at Bucharest
Last game: 22 June 1995 v. England at Pretoria

Philippe Sella was a dazzling centre whose flair could turn the course of any match in a moment. Famously described by the France coach Jacques Fouroux as having "the strength of a bull combined with the touch of a piano player", he made his debut as a 20-year-old against Romania in 1982 and became a permanent fixture of the French line-up for the next 13 years. With Sella and Serge Blanco directing operations in the backline, France became the kings of northern hemisphere rugby in the 1980s and thrilled rugby audiences around the world with their attacking, free-flowing play. In 1986, Sella became one of only four players in the history of the competition to score a try in all of his country's Five Nations matches in a season. He was appointed captain in 1992 and held the post until he retired from international rugby three years later with a then record number of caps to his name.

TOURIST INFORMATION

CITY BREAKS FOR THE INTREPID RUGBY TRAVELLER

As if being given the opportunity to watch the greatest rugby players battle it out over 44 days for the game's biggest prize wasn't enough, France 2007 will also provide you with a chance to explore some of Europe's most magical cities and provide memories from beyond the field of play that will last a lifetime. Here's a brief insight into what to expect…

Highlights
Eiffel Tower
Louvre
Arc de Triomphe
Champs Elysées
Musée d'Orsay
Père-Lachaise Cemetery
Montmartre
Notre Dame de Paris
Moulin Rouge
Jardin du Luxembourg

Tourist info
http://en.parisinfo.com/

PARIS
POPULATION: *2,152,000*

You could spend your entire life in Paris and, such is the variety of places to visit, still come no closer to a full understanding of the city. It is all things to all people: an artist's paradise; a fashionista's Shangri-La; a food lover's heaven. Most important of all, though, it's a great place to spend a few days and if you've never been before, here are a few of the things you simply have to do. Climb the Eiffel Tower: constructed in 1889, it is France's most-famous monument and a source of national pride; spend an afternoon in the Louvre, the world's greatest museum with an unparalleled collection of art; go to the Musée d'Orsay and see the world's finest collection of Impressionist art; take in the Notre Dame de Paris, home of the Hunchback and one of the finest examples of Gothic architecture anywhere on earth; take a stroll down the Champs Elysées and gaze in wonder at the magnificent Arc de Triomphe; take in the views of this wonderful city from the vantage point that is the Sacre Coeur, the highest point in Paris; take some time out in the Jardin du Luxembourg; visit the shrines of the famous in the extraordinary Père-Lachaise Cemetery; form your own opinion on the Pompidou Centre – Parisians either love it or hate it; spend an evening at the Moulin Rouge for a good old-fashioned knees-up; have lunch and take a stroll through the streets of Montmartre. And if you don't find the time to do any of the above, rest assured you'll be itching to come back for more.

↑ BORDEAUX

The undisputed wine capital of the world, Bordeaux – on the banks of the River Garonne, close to the Atlantic – is France's ninth biggest city and attracts 3 million visitors annually. The area boasts 13,000 grape growers, who farm 117,000 hectares of vineyards, and produce 700 million bottles of wine a year. The city oozes 18th-century grandeur with wide avenues, chic boutiques and ubiquitous cafés. Fascinating architecture is everywhere: the Pont de Pierre (above) – whose 17 arches span the Garonne, the magnificent Place de la Bourse, the Grand Théâtre, and magnificent churches, including the Cathédrale St-André and the St-Seurin, one of the city's most sacred sites. For museums, the Musée d'Aquitaine, Musée des Beaux-Arts and Musée des Arts Décoratifs are recommended.
Tourist info: *www.bordeaux.fr*

LENS

In 2008, Lens will be home to an annex of the Louvre museum. Until then, the town offers the shale heaps and brick-built miners' dwellings – known as *cités* or *corous* – from the town's coal-mining history. For war historians, Lens is close to many famous First World War sites, such as the national cemetery of Notre-Dame de Lorette – constructed along the Crêtes de Sacrifice (Trenches of Sacrifice) – and the village of Vimy, the site of the Canadian National Memorial. Visitors can explore the trenches themselves – even though the surrounding area is still littered with unexploded mines. Also nearby is Lille, with its old town, a mass of cobbled squares and narrow streets containing numerous shops, cafés and restaurants.
Tourist info: *www.ville-lens.fr*

↓ LYON

Lyon is the culinary capital of France. The old town, on the west bank of the River Saône, has narrow streets, lively cafés, tree-lined squares and superb medieval and Renaissance houses. Fourvière Hill – above the old town – was the nucleus of Roman Lyon. The sparkling white cathedral, the Basilique Notre-Dame de Fourvière (below), that casts its eye over the city is by a 2,000-year-old amphitheatre. Presqu'île – squeezed between the rivers Saône and Rhône – is the lively hub of central Lyon: including the beautiful Place des Terraux. North of Presqu'île is old Lyon, the former centre of the silk trade that generated the city's wealth. If you do nothing else, sample the culinary delights of one of the city's family-run bouchons.
Tourist info: *www.en.lyon-france.com*

MARSEILLE

France's second city and largest port, Marseille stands in stark contrast to the beauty of the Provence countryside around it. The city's ethnic mix adds to Marseille's overriding sense of colour and commotion. Dating back to 600 BC, when Phoenician Greeks sought shelter in Marseille's harbour, the *vieux port* is still a major attraction. Now a pleasure port with over 10,000 berths, it boasts a fish market, countless cafés and restaurants. Moving inland, visit: Boulevard Canebière, the once-grand rival to the Champs Elysées, now filled with banks and airline offices; for shopping, head towards Rue St-Ferréol and Rue Paradis; for architecture, try Notre-Dame-de-la-Garde, the neo-Byzantine basilica that dominates the city or the Cathédral de la Major, France's largest 19th-century church.
Tourist info: *www.marseille-tourisme.com*

MONTPELLIER

Set just inland from the Mediterranean and the capital of the Languedoc-Rousillon region, Montpellier is a lively city, dominated by student life – including France's oldest medical school (dating back to 1220). The old town, in the city centre, is where it all happens; the Place Jean-Jaurès, the liveliest square, is a market during the day and has lively outdoor-eating areas, bars and restaurants at night. Visit the city theatre in the Place de la Comédie – or L'Oeuf (The Egg) – its shape in the 18th century. Stroll through France's oldest garden – le Jardin des Plantes – founded in 1593, or take a stroll up to the Promenade de Peyrou and le Château d'Eau, from where you can see the sun as it sets over the Cévennes mountains.
Tourist info: *www.ot-montpellier.fr*

↗ NANTES

Nantes has been the Pays de la Loire's capital for 35 years but is emotionally and economically attached to Britanny. A commercial centre, thanks to its docks, it has a grisly past. The infamous pirate Bluebeard was burned at the stake here in 1440 and French slaves sailed to the Caribbean from Nantes for more than 200 years. Today, hi-tech industries blend with

lively pedestrian districts; tower blocks stand alongside cafés, the ultra-modern railway station complements wood-panelled houses on cobbled streets. Visit the 15th-century Château des Ducs de Bretagne (above), which was renovated in 2005 and now houses a museum. Of the other museums, the pick is the Musée Jules Verne, celebrating the life of the famous author, born in Nantes in 1828. If it's shopping you're after, head to the Bouffay quarter.

Tourist info: *www.nantes-tourisme.com*

ST-ETIENNE

Famous more for its football team than its natural beauty, St-Etienne has been one of France's most important industrial centres since coal was first mined there in the 12th century. But the city did not just make its name through coal: ribbon manufacture, armaments and steelworks gave the city its industrial reputation. Sadly, St-Etienne was extensively bombed in 1944 and was virtually flattened. But the rebuilt downtown area, around Place des Peuples, is lively and there are interesting museums. The Musée d'Art and d'Industrie covers the city's industrial background, and the Musée D'Art Moderne houses 20th-century works of art by Andy Warhol and Frank Stella. For natural beauty, take a short trip to Mont Pilat, a beautiful, pine-crested national park.

Tourist info: *www.tourisme-st-etienne.com*

TOULOUSE

Toulouse, in the southwest, has often been named France's favourite city. It is a thriving industrial hub, a major centre of education, boasts fine regional cuisine and quaint architecture. The city's major attraction is the cathedral, the Basilique St-Sernin, the world's largest Romanesque structure. Named after Toulouse's first saint – dragged to his death by a bull in 240 AD – parts are almost 1,000 years old. Also of interest are Le Capitole, the town hall, and, on the outskirts, the Cité de l'Espace – a park devoted to France's space programme, containing a full-size replica of Ariane V. For chic boutiques, head to Rue St Rome or Rue d'Alsace-Lorraine; for great nightlife, try Place du Président Wilson and Allée Roosevelt.

Tourist info: *www.toulouse.fr*

SPEAK THE LINGO

The travelling rugby supporter should be able to handle any situation that may arise on match day with tact and good humour by mastering these key French phrases …

* Can you tell me the way to the stadium, please?
* **Le stade, c'est par où s'il vous plaît ?**

* I've lost my ticket.
* **J'ai perdu mon billet.**

* What time's the kick-off?
* **Le coup d'envoi, c'est pour quelle heure ?**

* It's a lovely day for it!
* **Un vrai temps de rugbymen !**

* Excuse me. I think you're sitting in my seat.
* **Désolé, mais je crois que c'est ma place.**

* Would you mind sitting down please.
* **Vous pourriez vous asseoir s'il vous plaît ?**

* He's a big lad!
* **Il est balaise celui-là !**

* Kick it into touch!
* **Envoie-le en touche !**

* Go on Referee! A trip to the sin-bin should calm him down!
* **Allez l'arbitre ! Un petit tour en prison devrait le calmer !**

* A try and a conversion and we could still win it!
* **Un essai, une conversion et on peut encore gagner !**

* At the end of the day, rugby is the winner!
* **Au final, c'est une belle victoire pour le rugby !**

* Five large beers and a packet of nuts, please.
* **Cinq grandes bières et des cacahuètes s'il vous plaît.**

* Where are the toilets?
* **Où sont les toilettes s'il vous plaît ?**

* Can we have the rugby on the television, please, barman?
* **S'il vous plaît, barman, on peut regarder le rugby à la télé ?**

* And they'll be dancing in the streets of Montmartre, tonight!
* **Ca va être la fiesta dans les rues de Montmartre cette nuit !**

A TASTE OF FRANCE

FOOD AND DRINK

France 2007 will give you the opportunity to sample the world's most refined cuisine. The country that is home to some of the planet's most celebrated chefs offers a range of haute cuisine and provincial dishes that will leave you wanting to come back for more. Food and drink isn't merely sustenance in this country; it is a way of life.

FOOD

From fast food to the gastronomic experience of a lifetime, when the rugby is over and whatever your mood come the final whistle, the chances are you'll be heading for something to eat and the choice and variety in this country can be as bewildering as it can be divine. But before you get bemused by the choices on offer, the following is intended to give you a helping hand.

ON THE MENU

Bouillabaisse: traditional fish stew from the Provence region.
Cassoulet: slow-cooked stew with meat (often pork, duck, sausages), haricot beans and pork skin.
Confit de Canard: Gascony speciality of duck preserved in salt and cooked in its own fat.
Coq au Vin: chicken fricasseed in red wine with lardons, mushrooms and garlic.
Crêpes: very thin pancakes made with either savoury or sweet fillings.
Croque Monsieur: a type of toasted sandwich filled with ham and cheese.
Pot-au-feu: casserole dish, usually with beef and various root vegetables.
Ratatouille: vegetable stew from Provence.
Salade Niçoise: salad with vegetables, egg, anchovy, tuna and olive oil.
Steak au Poivre: a steak coated on one side with crushed peppercorns.

Typically a restaurant will offer you a choice of cheese. Often it's a local thing, with each area serving its regional specialities. At the last count there were more than 350 varieties of cheese in France, so there's plenty on offer.

FOR THE MORE ADVENTUROUS

The above dishes are all not only well known, but are also available in restaurants around the world. The following few simply haven't travelled in the same way. Can't understand why!

Escargot: exclusive restaurants in large cities sometimes have snails on their menu, in garlic or parsley butter, which should overpower any other taste.
Fois Gras: one of France's great delicacies. Pâté made from the liver of a fattened duck or goose.
Jambes des Grenouilles: literally, frogs' legs, this delicacy is not very common; its flavour has been likened to chicken.

DO IT YOURSELF

Walk through any village or small town in the morning and you will see literally dozens of locals walking around with a long, very thin, roll, called a baguette, and a carrier bag, inside of which will be the accompaniment for that day's lunch. These stores will sell you everything you need for a simple, quick, fresh lunch.

Boulangerie: bakery, selling wonderful baguettes and other types of bread.
Charcuterie: sells cooked meats, pâtés, etc.
Epicerie: grocers will offer, among other things, a choice of salads, vegetables, cold cooked meats and cheeses, all fresh that day.
Fromagerie: this cheese shop sells local, national and international varieties.
Patisserie: on sale here are incredible, not-so-low-calorie cakes and pastries.

DRINK

The French certainly know their wine. They have been producing it since Roman times and have been exporting it around the world since 1850; today the country is the world's largest wine producer by value. Enough books on the subject have been written to fill more than one library. For the visitor, there will always be plenty of choice. Here are just a few of the wines that even the French would go out of their way to taste:

SIX OF THE BEST REDS

Beaujolais: soft and fruity. *Look out for:* André Colonge, Aucoeur, Château de Pizay, Frédériquc Péroll.
Bordeaux: medium- to full-bodied. *Look out for:* Château Bonnet, Château Thieuley, Haut Bertinerie, Landereau.
Margaux: full-bodied, with a flagrant bouquet; one of the gems of French red wines. *Look out for:* Château d'Angludet, Desmirail, Giscours, La Tou de Mons.
Medoc: full-bodied and oak-aged, this is one of the most popular of French reds. *Look out for:* Canteloup, Greysac, La Tour-Haut-Caussan, Potensac.
Pauillac: full-bodied, with a bouquet of blackcurrants. *Look out for:* Château d'Armailhac, Fonbadet, Latour, Lafite-Rothschild, Pontet-Canet.

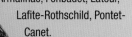

CHAMPAGNE

No trip to France would be complete without tasting the country's most revered product – the sparkling white wine produced in the Champagne region of northeast France and which takes its name. Although nobody quite knows how it was invented, the whole world is mighty glad that it was: produced from a blend of at least one of three grapes – chardonnay, pinot noir and meunier – more than 300 million bottles of fizz are produced every year, generating more than £4 billion revenue.

St Emilion: soft, medium-bodied and deep-flavoured. May be France's famous French red wine. *Look out for:* Beausejour, Beausejour-Becot, Belair, Canon, Fourtet, la Mondotte.

SIX FINE WHITES

Bordeaux: dry. *Look out for:* Aucoeur, André Colonge, Château de Pizay, Frédérique Péroll.

Chablis: dry and crisp. *Look out for:* Gilbert Picq, Jean Durup, Jean Dauvissat, Billaud-Simon, Jean Collet.

Muscat: produced with the perfect level of acidity. *Look out for:* Bruno Sorg, Ernest Burn, Hugel, Kitzler, Meyer-Fonné.

Pinot-Blanc: crisp and dry. *Look out for:* Cave de Turckheim, Henri Brecht, Kuentz-Bas, Meyer-Fonné, Paul Blanck, Zind Humbrecht.

Sancerre: pungent and dry. *Look out for:* Lucien Crochet, Pascal Jolivet, Serge Laporte, Vacheron, Vincent Pinard.

Sauternes: powerfully sweet dessert wine. *Look out for:* Les Justices, Clos Haut-Peyraguey, La Tour Blanche, D'Arche, Gilette, Haut-Bergerozn, Lamothe.

BEER AND CIDER

The French don't drink only wine and champagne, they drink beer, too, though not on the same scale as their neighbours in Germany, Belgium or England. And, especially in the north-west, they make some magnificent ciders. Here are a selection of best native beers and ciders:

Fischer Gold: a spring beer from France's largest independent brewery, with a soft, malty taste.

Jenlain: coming from nearer the Belgian border, this beer is opened as you would a champagne bottle, although the bubbles don't go up your nose like champagne.

Kronenbourg 1664: this beer is from Alsace region, near the German border; the influence is clear.

La Bio Jade: if you are going to Lens, then this is a local brew coming from the village Bénifontaine. It is a beautifully balanced organic beer, well worth trying.

Méteor: another beer from the Alsace region, it is the only French beer licensed to use the term Pilsner to describe the brewing method.

Domaine des Cinq Autels: an outstanding, dry organic cider from Normandy. Very refreshing on a hot early autumn day.

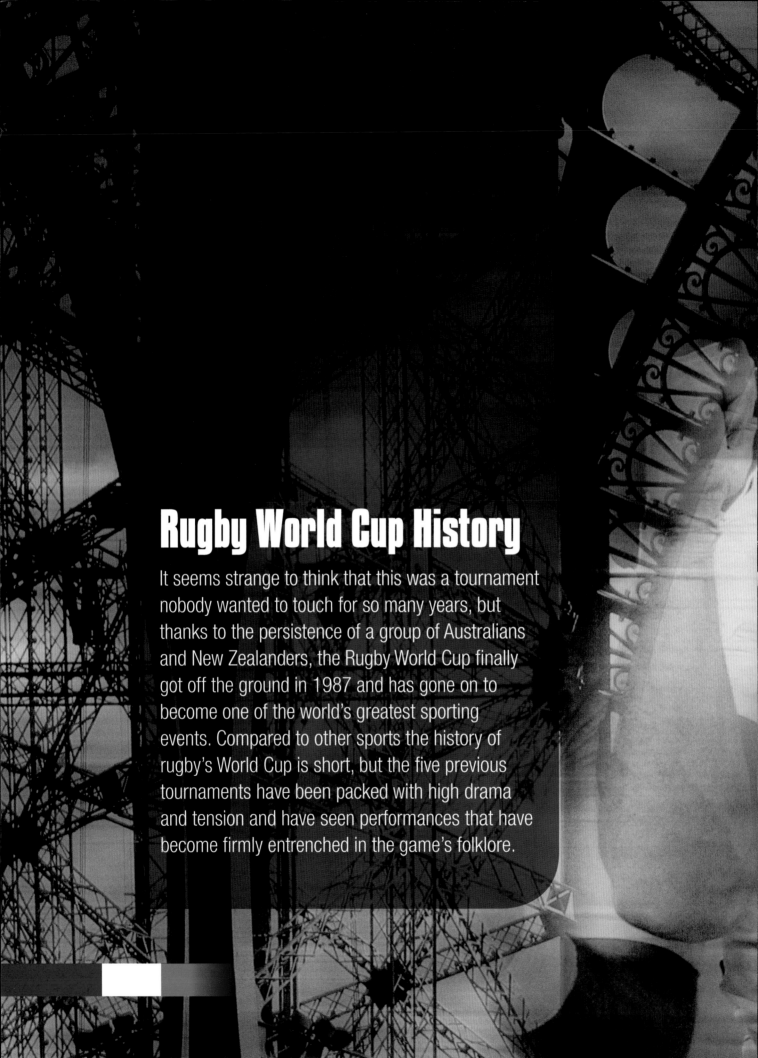

Rugby World Cup History

It seems strange to think that this was a tournament nobody wanted to touch for so many years, but thanks to the persistence of a group of Australians and New Zealanders, the Rugby World Cup finally got off the ground in 1987 and has gone on to become one of the world's greatest sporting events. Compared to other sports the history of rugby's World Cup is short, but the five previous tournaments have been packed with high drama and tension and have seen performances that have become firmly entrenched in the game's folklore.

WE ARE THE CHAMPIONS

In just 20 years the Rugby World Cup has become recognized as one of the world's premier sporting events. There have been five previous tournaments and four different nations have collected the Webb Ellis Trophy after the Final. Here is a chance to relive some of the memorable moments, matches and stars from the first five editions of the Rugby World Cup.

David Kirk: Bloodied and bruised he may have been, but the delight on the New Zealand captain's face is evident as he lifts the William Webb Ellis Trophy in front of an admiring Eden Park crowd.

1987 All Blacks on top Down Under

Hosts & Winners: **New Zealand**

The first Rugby World Cup was an invitation-only affair. The seven members of the IRB, plus those considered the nine strongest "other" rugby-playing nations, assembled in Australia and New Zealand to fight it out for the Webb Ellis Trophy.

It was a three-horse race from the start: Australia were playing the best rugby in the world; France were the undisputed kings of Europe; and New Zealand, reeling from the bans imposed on a number of their players following the unofficial 1986 Cavaliers tour of South Africa, still had the greatest pedigree in world rugby.

If the group stages were little more than a procession, then the quarter-finals also ran to form: New Zealand proved too strong for Scotland; France overcame Fiji; and Australia and Wales eased past Ireland and England, respectively. As the tournament came down to the last four, there was an overwhelming sense that it had only just begun.

New Zealand powered past Wales in the first semi-final, scoring eight tries en route to a 49–6 rout, but the real fireworks were reserved for the second semi-final. In what turned out to be the match of the tournament, Serge Blanco barrelled his way over the line in the last minute to earn France a shock win over pre-tournament favourites Australia. However, not for the first time in their World Cup history, France had reserved their best performance for the semi-finals. New Zealand were simply too good for them in the final and ran out 29–9 winners to send the Eden Park crowd home happy.

PLAYER OF THE TOURNAMENT

DAVID KIRK, 1987

Although he played only 17 Test matches, David Kirk left an indelible mark on the game. The Auckland scrum-half provided the vital cog in the All Blacks' sharp, mobile style of play and, with him at the helm, they romped to glory in the inaugural World Cup. He then led New Zealand to a famous Bledisloe Cup win over Australia in Sydney. A hamstring injury kept him out of action for most of 1987 and he then took up a Rhodes Scholarship at Oxford University. Now a successful businessman, he will forever be remembered as the first player to lift the Webb Ellis Trophy.

FOR THE RECORD, RWC 1987

QUARTER-FINALS
(Christchurch, Lancaster Park) **New Zealand 30, Scotland 3**
(Sydney, Concord Oval) **France 31, Fiji 16**
(Auckland, Eden Park) **Australia 33, Ireland 16**
(Brisbane, Ballymore) **Wales 16, England 3**

SEMI-FINALS
(Brisbane, Ballymore) **New Zealand 49, Wales 6**
(Sydney, Concord Oval) **France 30, Australia 24**

WORLD CUP FINAL
20 June 1987 at Eden Park, Auckland
NEW ZEALAND 29
Tries: Kirwan, Kirk, Jones;
Conversion: Fox; **Penalties:** Fox (4); **Drop-goal:** Fox
FRANCE 9
Try: Berbizier;
Conversion: Camberabero; **Penalty:** Camberabero

1991 Aussies show their resilience

Hosts: England
Winners: Australia

It was the northern hemisphere's turn to host the tournament four years later. With the eight quarter-finalists from 1987 gaining automatic qualification to the tournament, 32 teams were invited to fight it out for the remaining eight World Cup spots. The outcome was that Western Samoa replaced Tonga in an otherwise unchanged line-up from 1987. And what an impact they made, defeating Wales 16–13 in their opening game and following that up with a victory over Argentina to condemn the Welsh to an early tournament exit. But that was the end of the shocks. Just as had been the case four years earlier, the gulf between the established nations and the emerging ones was vast.

There were, however, some interesting quarter-final clashes. England came through a tense encounter against France in Paris; the Irish fell to a last-minute Australian try in Dublin; Scotland had too much for Western Samoa; and defending champions New Zealand fought off some dogged Canadian resistance to ease through to the last four.

The semi-finals seemed like a reunion of old friends. In Edinburgh, a last-gasp Rob Andrew drop-goal was enough for England to see off the Auld Enemy, and Australia showed all their class to defeat archrivals New Zealand 16–6 in Dublin. The Wallabies looked like the team to beat. And England, roared on by a partisan Twickenham crowd, did all they could to do so. However, after scoring an early try through Tony Daly, Australia repelled wave after wave of English attacks to run out 12–6 winners and claim the trophy for the first time.

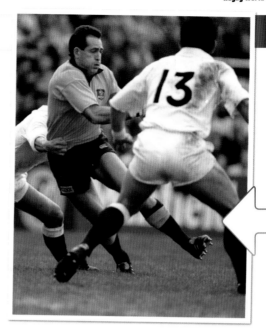

David Campese: He did not score in the 1991 World Cup final, but many believe the Australian winger contributed to England's downfall with his pre-match comments about their "one-dimensional play". England abandoned their forward-dominated style but, try as they might, could not penetrate the Wallabies' defence.

PLAYER OF THE TOURNAMENT

DAVID CAMPESE, 1991

Although he has as many critics as admirers, David Campese is the best rugby player Australia has produced. He made a try-scoring debut against New Zealand in 1982 and crossed the line again in his second match. He made his name on Australia's Grand Slam-winning tour to the British Isles in 1984, thrilling the crowd with a magnificent solo try against the Barbarians. The highlight of his career came with Australia's 1991 World Cup, when his six tries saw him voted player of the tournament. He retired in 1996 with 101 caps and a then world record 64 tries to his name.

FOR THE RECORD, RWC 1991

QUARTER-FINALS
(Edinburgh, Murrayfield) **Scotland 28, Western Samoa 6**
(Paris, Parc des Princes) **England 19, France 10**
(Dublin, Lansdowne Road) **Australia 19, Ireland 18**
(Paris, Stade du Nord) **New Zealand 29, Canada 13**

SEMI-FINALS
(Edinburgh, Murrayfield) **England 9, Scotland 6**
(Dublin, Lansdowne Road) **Australia 16, New Zealand 6**

WORLD CUP FINAL
2 November 1991 at Twickenham
AUSTRALIA 12
Try: Daly; **Conversion:** Lynagh; **Penalties:** Lynagh (2)
ENGLAND 6
Penalties: Webb (2)

1995 Joy for the Rainbow Nation

Hosts and winners: South Africa

The year the World Cup truly came of age turned out to be a highly emotional, month-long celebration of South Africa's return to the international rugby fold. Their opening 27–18 victory over Australia in Cape Town meant that the tournament's touch paper was lit from the word go and the group stages were dotted with fantastic performances, including the emergence of Jonah Lomu, New Zealand's bulldozer of a wing. However, they were also tinged with tragedy of the highest order when Ivory Coast's Max Brito was paralysed in the opening moments of his country's match against Tonga.

The top eight seeds all made it through to the quarter-finals. This time, though, they were last-eight match-ups with spice. France ended Ireland's interest in the tournament; South Africa had too much for Western Samoa; England's Rob Andrew found his last-minute kicking boots for the second tournament in a row to end Australia's reign; and New Zealand ended Scotland's plucky resistance with a 48–30 victory.

South Africa continued their march to the final with a stubborn win over France, but it was the manner of New Zealand's semi-final win over England that got everyone talking. Jonah Lomu bullied his way over the line four times as England found themselves on the wrong end of a 45–29 hammering. If South Africa wanted to win the tournament, they would have to find a way of stopping Lomu. They did, albeit courtesy of a Joel Stransky drop-goal in extra time, and as Nelson Mandela, wearing a replica No. 6 Springbok shirt, handed the trophy to François Pienaar, you got the sense that the party had just started.

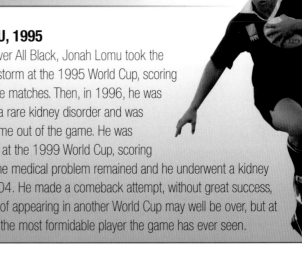

PLAYER OF THE TOURNAMENT

JONAH LOMU, 1995

The youngest-ever All Black, Jonah Lomu took the rugby world by storm at the 1995 World Cup, scoring seven tries in five matches. Then, in 1996, he was diagnosed with a rare kidney disorder and was forced to take time out of the game. He was back to his best at the 1999 World Cup, scoring eight tries, but the medical problem remained and he underwent a kidney transplant in 2004. He made a comeback attempt, without great success, and his dreams of appearing in another World Cup may well be over, but at his best he was the most formidable player the game has ever seen.

World Cup magic moment: A Hollywood script-writer could not have come up with a better finale. The image of Nelson Mandela handing the World Cup to South Africa's winning captain, François Pienaar, both men wearing the South Africa No. 6 shirt, will live long in the memories of all who witnessed it.

1999 France run out of steam as Aussies triumph

Final Host: **Wales**
Winners: **Australia**

The success of the previous tournament was reflected in the corporate success of the 1999 edition of the World Cup. Global television viewing figures passed the three billion mark for the first time and profits from the tournament rose from £17.6 million in 1995 to £47 million. Unfortunately, it couldn't be said that it was triple the fun on the field of play.

With the tournament entry increased to 20, an unusual format was employed to get eight quarter-finalists. The five winners qualified of right, but the five group runners-up plus the best third-placed team fought it out in a round of three play-off matches for the final three quarter-final berths. This extra stage gave the 1999 World Cup a somewhat drawn-out feel. Not for the first time, the tournament really started only when the 20 teams had been whittled down to eight, and following the quarter-finals South Africa, Australia, France and New Zealand found themselves in the semi-final shake-up.

Both semi-finals were staged at Twickenham, and in the first of them Australia faced a kicking encounter against South Africa and emerged 27–21 winners. The real fireworks were reserved for the second semi, and in what proved the match of the tournament, underdogs France produced 20

minutes of scintillating second-half rugby to stun the All Blacks 43–31.

But just as had been the case 12 years earlier, France had reserved their best performance for the last four. In a one-sided final in Cardiff, tries from Ben Tune and Owen Finnegan, coupled with the precise boot of Matt Burke, saw Australia ease to a 35–12 victory to lift the cup for the second time.

Captain Fantastic: John Eales collected his second World Cup-winner's medal and became the second Wallaby to lift the World Cup when Australia routed France in the 1999 final in Cardiff.

FOR THE RECORD, RWC 1995

QUARTER-FINALS
(Durban, King's Park) **France 36, Ireland 12**
(Johannesburg, Ellis Park) **South Africa 42, Samoa 14**
(Cape Town, Newlands) **England 25, Australia 22**
(Pretoria, Loftus Versfeld) **New Zealand 48, Scotland 20**

SEMI-FINALS
(Durban, King's Park) **South Africa 19, France 15**
(Cape Town, Newlands) **New Zealand 45, England 29**

WORLD CUP FINAL
24 June 1995 at Ellis Park, Johannesburg
SOUTH AFRICA 15
Penalties: Stransky (3); **Drop-goals:** Stransky (2)
NEW ZEALAND 12
Penalties: Mehrtens (3); **Drop-goal:** Mehrtens

FOR THE RECORD RWC 1999

QUARTER-FINALS
(Cardiff, Millennium) **Australia 24, Wales 9**
(Paris, Stade de France) **South Africa 44, England 21**
(Dublin, Lansdowne Road) **France 47, Argentina 26**
(Edinburgh, Murrayfield) **New Zealand 30, Scotland 18**

SEMI-FINALS
(Twickenham) **Australia 27, South Africa 21**
(Twickenham) **France 43, New Zealand 31**

WORLD CUP FINAL
Millennium Stadium, Cardiff
AUSTRALIA 35
Tries: Tune, Finnegan;
Conversions: Burke (2); **Penalties:** Burke (7)
FRANCE 12
Penalties: Lamaison (4)

PLAYER OF THE TOURNAMENT

JOHN EALES, 1999

John Eales is the most successful captain in the history of Australian rugby. One of only five players to have won the World Cup twice, he ended his career at eighth on the Australian all-time points-scoring list, a phenomenal achievement for a lock forward, but he was a goal-kicker for a period. He made his Test debut in 1991 as a 21-year-old and played a full part in his side's World Cup victory that year. Five years later he was made Australian captain. He suffered a serious shoulder injury early in 1999 and fought his way back into the side that lifted the World Cup in 1999.

2003 Wilkinson kicks England to victory

Hosts: **Australia**
Winners: **England**

With more spectators than ever before and with record global viewing figures, rugby's premier event had finally arrived on the world's sporting stage. Originally planned as an event to be staged in both Australia and New Zealand, a row between the All Blacks rugby board and the World Cup organizers left Australia as sole host.

The format issues of the previous World Cup had been ironed out: sensibly, it was decided that the 20 teams would be split into four groups of five with the top two from each group progressing to the quarter-finals. As expected, the top eight seeds emerged from the group stages and, in a tournament that was yielding few surprises, the top-four ranked nations in world rugby – Australia, England, France and New Zealand – made it through to the semi-finals with relative ease.

But then Australia sprang the first major surprise of the tournament, dashing the hopes of co-favourites New Zealand with a shock 22–10 win in Sydney. A day later, at the same venue, the second semi-final played more to the formbook, with Jonny Wilkinson kicking all of England's points in their 24–7 win over France.

The major surprise of the final was that Australia pushed England so close. In a dramatic encounter, the sides went into extra-time with the scores locked at 14–14. With the clock ticking down into the final seconds of the match, with both sides having added a penalty, Wilkinson unleashed his left boot and dropped a goal to secure England a memorable victory.

Joy unconfined: Martin Johnson became the first player from the northern hemisphere to lift the World Cup when England triumphed over Australia in 2003.

PLAYER OF THE TOURNAMENT

JONNY WILKINSON, 2003

Renowned for his obsessive approach to practice, Jonny Wilkinson made his England debut against Ireland as an 18-year-old in 1998. He made his World Cup debut a year later, and many blame his non-selection for England's quarter-final defeat to South Africa. But it was his performances during the 2003 World Cup that created his legend. The metronomic accuracy of his boot, allied to England's forward muscularity, took England to World Cup glory and his match-winning drop-goal will be etched in the memories of every England supporter. Sadly, a series of injuries meant that he didn't appear in an England shirt until early 2007. How badly England fans missed him.

FOR THE RECORD, RWC 2003

QUARTER-FINALS
(Melbourne, Telstra Dome) **New Zealand 29, South Africa 9**
(Brisbane, Suncorp Stadium) **Australia 33, Scotland 16**
(Melbourne, Telstra Dome) **France 43, Ireland 21**
(Brisbane, Suncorp Stadium) **England 28, Wales 17**

SEMI-FINALS
(Sydney, Telstra Stadium) **Australia, 22 New Zealand 10**
(Sydney, Telstra Stadium) **England 24, France 7**

WORLD CUP FINAL
22 November 2003 at Telstra Stadium, Sydney
ENGLAND 20
Try: Robinson; **Penalties:** Wilkinson (4); **Drop-goal:** Wilkinson
AUSTRALIA 17
Try: Tuqiri; **Penalties:** Flatley (4)

World Cup Records

Records are there to be broken, be they good or bad, cherished or unwanted, memorable or instantly forgettable. The first five World Cups have seen some spectacular rugby, with many of the performers firmly establishing themselves in the pantheon of rugby greats, but who has scored more tries than any other player, which team has the best winning record, who has won by the biggest winning margin and which team holds the record for conceding the most points? Which player has kicked the most drop-goals? Who has slotted the most penalties or conversions? Who has scored more points than any other player in the history of the World Cup? The answers to these and many other questions lie in the following pages, which show a complete record of both team and individual records through all five World Cups ...

WORLD CUP RECORDS

COMPLETE TEAM RECORDS

TEAM	P	W	D	L	PF	PA	W.%
New Zealand	31	26	0	5	1384	457	83.9
Australia	29	24	0	5	987	380	82.8
South Africa	17	14	0	3	556	247	82.3
France	29	22	1	6	968	543	77.6
England	28	20	0	8	957	458	71.4
Scotland	24	14	1	9	770	486	60.4
Wales	21	12	0	9	523	454	57.1
Ireland	21	11	0	10	610	446	52.4
Samoa	16	8	0	8	425	416	50.0
Canada	17	6	0	11	336	419	35.3
Argentina	18	6	0	12	433	439	33.3
Fiji	15	5	0	10	345	422	33.3
Italy	16	5	0	11	278	599	31.3
Uruguay	7	2	0	5	98	352	28.6
Romania	16	4	0	12	221	609	25.0
USA	13	2	0	11	201	472	15.3
Tonga	13	2	0	11	166	537	15.3
Japan	16	1	0	15	295	765	6.3
Spain	3	0	0	3	18	122	0.0
Ivory Coast	3	0	0	3	29	172	0.0
Georgia	4	0	0	4	46	200	0.0
Zimbabwe	6	0	0	6	84	309	0.0
Namibia	7	0	0	7	70	496	0.0

MOST POINTS IN A MATCH BY A TEAM
145	New Zealand v. Japan, Bloemfontein	4 June 1995
142	Australia v. Namibia, Adelaide	25 October 2003
111	England v. Uruguay, Brisbane	2 November 2003
101	New Zealand v. Italy, Huddersfield	14 October 1999
101	England v. Tonga, Twickenham	15 October 1999
91	New Zealand v. Tonga, Brisbane	24 October 2003
90	Australia v. Romania, Brisbane	18 October 2003
89	Scotland v. Ivory Coast, Rustenburg	26 May 1995
84	England v. Georgia, Perth	12 October 2003
74	New Zealand v. Fiji, Christchurch	27 May 1987

BIGGEST WINNING MATCH MARGINS
142	Australia 142–0 Namibia, Adelaide	25 October 2003
128	New Zealand 145–17 Japan, Bloemfontein	4 June 1995
98	England 111–13 Uruguay, Brisbane	2 November 2003
98	New Zealand 101–3 Italy, Huddersfield	14 October 2003
91	England 101–10 Tonga, Twickenham	15 October 1999
89	Scotland 89–0 Ivory Coast, Rustenburg	26 May 1995

MOST TRIES IN A MATCH BY ONE TEAM
22	Australia 142–0 Namibia, Adelaide	25 October 2003
21	New Zealand 145–17 Japan, Bloemfontein	4 June 1995
17	England 111–13 Uruguay, Brisbane	2 November 2003
14	New Zealand 101–3 Italy, Huddersfield	14 October 1999
13	England 101–10 Tonga, Twickenham	15 October 1999
13	Scotland 89–0 Ivory Coast, Rustenburg	26 May 1995
13	France 70–12 Zimbabwe, Auckland	2 June 1987

INDIVIDUAL

MOST POINTS IN ONE COMPETITION
Points	Name	Country	Year	Breakdown
126	Grant Fox	New Zealand	1987	21p, 30c 1dg
113	Jonny Wilkinson	England	2003	23p, 10c, 8dg
112	Thierry Lacroix	France	1995	4t, 26p, 7c
104	Gavin Hastings	Scotland	1995	5t, 17p, 14c
103	Frédéric Michalak	France	2003	2t, 18p, 18c, 1dg
102	Gonzalo Quesada	Argentina	1999	31p, 3c, 1dg
101	Matt Burke	Australia	1999	2t, 19p, 17c
100	Elton Flatley	Australia	2003	1t, 21p, 16c

MOST POINTS IN A MATCH BY A PLAYER
45	(1t, 20c) Simon Culhane, New Zealand v. Japan, Bloemfontein	4 June 1995
44	(4t, 2p, 9c) Gavin Hastings, Scotland v. Ivory Coast, Rustenburg	26 May 1995
42	(2t, 16c) Mat Rogers, Australia v. Namibia, Adelaide	25 Oct 2003
36	(1t, 11c, 3p) Tony Brown, New Zealand v. Italy, Huddersfield	14 Oct 1999
36	(4p, 12c) Paul Grayson, England v. Tonga, Twickenham	15 Oct 1999
34	(1t, 4p, 1c, 5d) Jannie de Beer, South Africa v. England, Paris	24 Oct 1999
32	(1t, 5p, 6c) Jonny Wilkinson, England v. Italy, Twickenham	2 Oct 1999

MOST TRIES IN ONE TOURNAMENT
8	Jonah Lomu, New Zealand	1999
7	Marc Ellis, New Zealand	1995
7	Doug Howlett, New Zealand	2003
7	Jonah Lomu, New Zealand	1995
7	Mils Muliaina, New Zealand	2003

MOST TRIES IN A MATCH BY A PLAYER
6	Marc Ellis, New Zealand 145–17 Japan, Bloemfontein	4 June 1995
5	Chris Latham, Australia 142–0 Namibia, Adelaide	25 October 2003
5	Josh Lewsey, England 111–13 Uruguay, Brisbane	2 November 2003
4	Keith Wood, Ireland 53–8 USA, Dublin	2 October 1999
4	Gavin Hastings, Scotland 89–0 Ivory Coast, Rustenburg	26 May 1995
4	Chester Williams, South Africa 42–14 Samoa, Johannesburg	10 June 1995
4	Jonah Lomu, New Zealand 45–29 England, Cape Town	18 June 1995
4	Brian Robinson, Ireland 55–11 Zimbabwe, Dublin	6 October 1991
4	Ieuan Evans, Wales 40–9 Canada, Invercargill	3 June 1987
4	Craig Green, New Zealand 74–13 Fiji, Christchurch	27 May 1987
4	John Gallagher, New Zealand 74–13 Fiji, Christchurch	27 May 1987

MOST APPEARANCES
22	Jason Leonard, England	1991–2003
18	Martin Johnson, England	1991–2003
17	Sean Fitzpatrick, New Zealand	1987–95

FOUR WORLD CUP FINALS SQUADS
Gareth Rees, Canada	1987–1999
Al Charron, Canada	1991–2003
Carlo Checchinato, Italy	1991–2003
Fabien Galthié, France (pictured, right)	1991–2003
Martin Johnson, England	1991–2003
Jason Leonard, England	1991–2003
Brian Lima, Samoa	1991–2003
Pedro Sporleder, Argentina	1991–2003

MOST CONVERSIONS IN A MATCH

20	Simon Culhane, New Zealand v. Japan, Bloemfontein	4 June 1995
16	Mat Rogers, Australia v. Namibia, Adelaide	25 October 2003
12	Paul Grayson, England v. Tonga, Twickenham	15 October 1999
12	Leon McDonald, New Zealand v. Tonga, Brisbane	24 October 2003
11	Tony Brown, New Zealand v. Italy, Huddersfield	14 October 1999
11	Elton Flatley, Australia v. Romania, Brisbane	18 October 2003
11	Paul Grayson, England v. Uruguay, Brisbane	2 November 2003
10	Grant Fox, New Zealand v. Fiji, Christchurch	27 May 1987

MOST PENALTIES IN A MATCH

8	Matt Burke, Australia v. South Africa, Twickenham	30 October 1999
8	Gavin Hastings, Scotland v. Tonga, Pretoria	30 May 1995
8	Thierry Lacroix, France v. Ireland, Durban	10 June 1995
8	Gonzalo Quesada, Argentina v. Samoa, Llanelli	10 October 1999

MOST PENALTIES IN ONE TOURNAMENT

31	Gonzalo Quesada, Argentina (pictured above, far left, No. 10)	1999
26	Thierry Lacroix, France	1995
23	Jonny Wilkinson, England	2003
21	Elton Flatley, Australia	2003
21	Grant Fox, New Zealand	1987
20	Rob Andrew, England	1995

MOST DROP-GOALS IN A MATCH

5	Jannie de Beer, South Africa v. England, Paris	24 October 1999
3	Jonny Wilkinson, England v. France, Sydney	16 November 2003

MOST TRIES

Team	Tries
New Zealand	184
Australia	122
France	115
England	99
Scotland	94
Ireland	71
Wales	63
South Africa	61
Samoa	53
Argentina	40

MOST CONVERSIONS

Team	Cons
New Zealand	137
Australia	93
France	79
England	76
Scotland	66
Ireland	55
Wales	45
South Africa	43
Samoa	36
Fiji	27

MOST PENALTIES

Team	Pens
England	98
France	86
New Zealand	78
Australia	74
Scotland	64
Argentina	58
Ireland	50
South Africa	43
Wales	41
Canada	40

MOST DROP-GOALS

Team	DGs
England	14
South Africa	12
France	8
Ireland	7
Canada	6
Fiji	6
New Zealand	6
Scotland	6
Wales	6
Argentina	5

RUGBY WORLD CUP INDIVIDUAL LEADERS

MOST OVERALL POINTS

Points	Name	Country	Years	Breakdown
227	Gavin Hastings	Scotland	1987–95	9t, 36p, 39c
195	Michael Lynagh	Australia	1987–95	4t, 33p, 36c, 2dg
182	Jonny Wilkinson	England	1999–2003	1t, 39p, 18c, 8dg
170	Grant Fox	New Zealand	1987–91	31p, 37c, 1dg
163	Andrew Mehrtens	New Zealand	1995–99	1t, 33p, 25c, 3dg
135	Gonzalo Quesada	Argentina	1999–2003	35p, 12c, 2dg
125	Matt Burke	Australia	1987–95	6t, 19p, 19c
124	Thierry Lacroix	France	1991–95	4t, 30p, 7c
120	Gareth Rees	Canada	1987–99	25p, 15c, 5dg

MOST TRIES

Name	Country	Years	Tries
Jonah Lomu	New Zealand	1995–99	15
Rory Underwood	England	1991–95	11
David Campese	Australia	1987–91	10
Brian Lima	Samoa	1991–99	10
Gavin Hastings	Scotland	1987–95	9
Jeff Wilson	New Zealand	1995–99	9
8 players			7

MOST PENALTIES

Name	Country	Years	Pens
Jonny Wilkinson	England	1999–2003	39
Gavin Hastings	Scotland	1987–95	36
Gonzalo Quesada	Argentina	1999–2003	35
Michael Lynagh	Australia	1987–95	33
Andrew Mehrtens	New Zealand	1995–99	33
Grant Fox	New Zealand	1987–91	31
Thierry Lacroix	France	1991–95	30
Gareth Rees	Canada	1987–99	25
Elton Flatley	Australia	2003	21
Jonathan Webb	England	1987–91	21

MOST CONVERSIONS

Name	Country	Years	Cons
Gavin Hastings	Scotland	1987–95	39
Grant Fox	New Zealand	1987–91	37
Michael Lynagh	Australia	1987–95	36
Paul Grayson	England	1999–2003	27
Andrew Mehrtens	New Zealand	1995–99	25
Simon Culhane	New Zealand	1995	20
Leon MacDonald	New Zealand	2003	20
Matt Burke	Australia	1987–95	19
Didier Camberabero	France	1987–91	19
Dan Carter	New Zealand	2003	19
Neil Jenkins	Wales	1995–99	19

MOST DROP-GOALS

Name	Country	Years	DGs
Jonny Wilkinson	England	1999–2003	8
Jannie De Beer	South Africa	1999	6
Rob Andrew	England	1991–95	5
Gareth Rees	Canada	1987–99	5
Jonathan Davies	Wales	1987	3
Andrew Mehrtens	New Zealand	1995–99	3
Joel Stransky	South Africa	1995	3
Gregor Townsend	Scotland	1999	3
10 players			2

RUGBY TERMINOLOGY

SCRUM DOWN FOR THE RUGBY WORLD CUP

For the uninitiated armchair follower, watching a game of rugby featuring your favourite team can be a confusing affair as well as an exhilarating one. Here is a quick explanation of a few of the terms and phrases you can expect to hear when watching the 2007 World Cup on your television screens. If you do your homework now, your whole viewing experience will be altogether more pleasurable.

5-METRE SCRUM

An attacking position which is caused by either a defending player going back into his own in-goal area and being tackled or losing the ball, or if the defending side stops the opposition from scoring within five metres of the try-line, but doesn't force a turnover.

22

A line on a rugby pitch 22 metres from the goal-line. A kick from the defending team in this area does not have to bounce in the field of play for the line-out to be thrown in where the ball went out of play.

22 DROP-OUT

A drop-kick to the defensive team to restart the game taken on the 22-metre line.

ADVANTAGE

Following a penalty or scrum award, the offended-against team may retain possession of the ball and score; if no advantage accrues, the referee will go back to his previous decision. The referee will hold his arm out to show the advantage is still in progress.

BLOOD BIN

If a player is bleeding and needs treatment off the field, a temporary replacement can come on in his place.

CONVERSION

A bonus kick for two points after a side has scored a try. The kick must be taken from a point in a direct line parallel to the touchline from where the player touched down for a try in the in-goal area.

DROP-GOAL

A successful field goal worth three points resulting from a successful drop-kick.

DROP-KICK

A kick made when the ball rebounds from the ground after dropping from the hand.

FEEDING

An offence whereby the scrum-half "feeds" the ball to his hooker at a scrum, rather than to a point between both hookers. If found guilty, the referee will award a free-kick to the opposing team.

FORWARD PASS

A pass that is deemed to have gone forward. The referee will call for a scrum at the point of the offence, and possession will pass to the other side.

FREE-KICK

A free-kick is awarded to a side if their opponents are deemed to have committed an offence not serious enough to warrant a penalty. The side may call for a kick (although they will not retain possession of the ball should it find touch) or a scrum (for which they will retain possession of the ball).

HOSPITAL PASS

You are standing next to the touchline with nowhere to go. Your opponents' burly prop and irate, adrenaline-fuelled flanker are so close you can hear them snarl. Your team-mate chooses that moment to pass you the ball. You are flattened within milliseconds of catching it and then spend interminable seconds, at the bottom of a pile of foraging bodies, fighting for breath. You have been the victim of a hospital pass.

IN-GOAL AREA

An area between the try-line and the end-line, inside which area the attacking team must ground the ball to score a try.

JUMPER

An especially tall player, often over 2m tall, normally a second- or back-row forward, who is lifted at a line-out to catch in the incoming throw.

KNOCK-ON

When the ball is dropped or knocked forward by a player either in possession or actively attempting to gain possession, the referee will award a scrum to the opposition at the point of the infringement.

LINE-OUT

A method of restarting play after the ball has been kicked into touch. The opposing forwards form a line at the point where the ball went into touch. The ball is thrown in and the forwards compete for the ball. There must be a minimum of two players in the line-out.

(Left) Scrum: Ireland and Wales go head to head in a scrum during the 2007 Six Nations.
(Opposite below) Line-out: Ireland's Paul O'Connell displays the perfect line-out technique receiving a throw against England during the 2007 Six Nations.

MARK

A call used by a defender in his own 22 who has successfully caught an opponent's kick which has not bounced. The defensive team is awarded a free-kick.

MAUL

A loose scrum formed when two sides are trying to gain possession of a ball that is being held above the ground.

OFFSIDE

Marked by an imaginary line from the defenders' last foot in a scrum, ruck or maul, ten yards from a line-out or a kick, or from behind the try-line if an attacking side is within ten yards of it, if a player breaches this line he will be deemed offside. If a player in an offside position cannot avoid being struck by the ball, then the referee will rule an accidental offside and award a scrum to the opposing team.

PENALTY

A referee will award a penalty to a side if their opponents breach the rules. They will be asked whether they would like to run with the ball, take a kick or form a scrum at the point of the infringement. The attacking side may kick for touch (for which they will retain possession of the ball for the ensuing line-out) or for goal (for which they will receive three points if successful). If they opt for a scrum, they will have the put-in. If they decide to run, only defensive players

ten metres downfield from the mark of the offence – or on the goal-line – can move forward to tackle the ball-carrier.

PENALTY TRY

A try awarded by the referee after the defending team deliberately or continuously commits an offence to stop a try being scored. The conversion is always from in front of the posts.

PUT-IN

The possession of the ball for the scrum.

RED CARD

see Sent off.

REPLACEMENT

A substitute can replace any player who leaves the field for either an injury or tactical reason. Although no direct replacement can be made for a player shown either a red or yellow card, for set-scrums a replacement prop or hooker can come on to the field – temporarily in the event of a sin-binning – taking over from another forward or a back.

RUCK

A loose scrum formed when two sides are trying to gain possession of a ball that is on the ground.

SCRUM

A contest between the two packs of forwards for possession of the ball. One of the teams will have been awarded the put-in.

SENT OFF

If a player commits a particularly violent or

malicious offence, the referee can show him a red card and send him from the field for the remainder of the match.

SIN BIN

If a player commits a deliberate offence to stop or slow the attacking team's momentum, the referee may show the offender a yellow card, sending off the player for ten minutes.

"TAP AND GO"

Occurs, following a penalty, when a player taps the ball with his foot over the point of the infringement. Play has then restarted.

TMO (TELEVISION MATCH OFFICIAL)

The match official in the stands with access to television replays. A referee will call a TMO for confirmation on whether or not to award a try.

TRY

An award of five points for when a player crosses the opponent's try-line and touches the ball down in the in-goal area.

TURNOVER

When a side enters a ruck or maul and loses possession of the ball.

UP-AND-UNDER

A high kick used to put pressure on an opponent's defence. A perfect up-and-under will see a team's attack run towards the opponents' defence and compete for the ball as it lands.

YELLOW CARD

see Sin bin.

RUGBY WORLD CUP QUIZ

QUESTION TIME

So you think you know your rugby? Here are 20 questions that will test the knowledge of even the savviest of rugby fans:

1. Who, in 1987, was the first captain to lift the World Cup?
2. Who was the leading points scorer in the 1987 World Cup?
3. Which team scored 22 tries in a match against Namibia in the 2003 World Cup?
4. Who captained Australia to victory in the 1991 World Cup?
5. Who scored a World Cup record six tries in a match in South Africa 1995?
6. Who is the leading points scorer in the history of the World Cup?
7. Who has scored the most World Cup tries?
8. Who holds the record for the most drop-goals in a World Cup match?
9. Who has played in more World Cup matches than any other player?
10. Who was the leading points scorer in the 1991 World Cup?
11. Who was the leading points scorer in the 1995 World Cup?
12. Who scored all of South Africa's points in their successful World Cup final clash against New Zealand?
13. Which two players, other than Jonah Lomu, have scored ten or more tries in the World Cup?
14. Who holds the record for the most points scored in a World Cup match?
15. Which country holds the record for the most consecutive losses in the World Cup finals?
16. Who was the leading points scorer at the 1999 World Cup?
17. Which stadium holds the attendance record for a World Cup match?
18. Which All Black player scored the World Cup's first-ever try back in 1987?
19. Who was the leading points scorer at the 2003 World Cup?
20. Name the two try scorers in the 2003 World Cup final.

PICTURE QUIZ

1. **MYSTERY PLAYERS**
   Never mind the ball ... let's get on with the game!
   Can you identify these uncharacteristically shy-and-retiring ruckers and maulers?

2. **SAY IT WITH FLOWERS**
   It's enough to make you want to break out into a chorus of "Flowers of Scotland".
   Which countries' fans will be wearing these luscious blooms in their lapels during the Rugby World Cup?

3. **SPOTTER'S GUIDE**
   What magnificent beasts they are ...
   Which countries are nicknamed after these furry and feathery friends?

1. MYSTERY PLAYERS

2. SAY IT WITH FLOWERS

3. SPOTTER'S GUIDE

FILL-IN TOURNAMENT CHART

All kick-offs listed in local French time

GROUP A

Date	Match			Venue	Time	Result
8 September	England	v.	USA	Lens	18:00	...–...
9 September	South Africa	v.	Samoa	Paris	16:00	...–...
12 September	USA	v.	Tonga	Montpellier	14:00	...–...
14 September	England	v.	South Africa	St Denis	21:00	...–...
16 September	Samoa	v.	Tonga	Montpellier	16:00	...–...
22 September	South Africa	v.	Tonga	Lens	14:00	...–...
22 September	England	v.	Samoa	Nantes	16:00	...–...
26 September	Samoa	v.	USA	St Etienne	20:00	...–...
28 September	England	v.	Tonga	Paris	21:00	...–...
30 September	South Africa	v.	USA	Montpellier	20:00	...–...

Final Group A table

	P	W	L	D	PF	PA	Pts
A1							
A2							
A3							
A4							
A5							

GROUP B

Date	Match			Venue	Time	Result
8 September	Australia	v.	Japan	Lyon	15:45	...–...
9 September	Wales	v.	Canada	Nantes	14:00	...–...
12 September	Japan	v.	Fiji	Toulouse	18:00	...–...
15 September	Wales	v.	Australia	Cardiff	15:00	...–...
16 September	Fiji	v.	Canada	Cardiff	14:00	...–...
20 September	Wales	v.	Japan	Cardiff	21:00	...–...
23 September	Australia	v.	Fiji	Montpellier	14:30	...–...
25 September	Canada	v.	Japan	Bordeaux	18:00	...–...
29 September	Australia	v.	Canada	Bordeaux	15:00	...–...
29 September	Wales	v.	Fiji	Nantes	17:00	...–...

Final Group B table

	P	W	L	D	PF	PA	Pts
B1							
B2							
B3							
B4							
B5							

GROUP C

Date	Match			Venue	Time	Result
8 September	New Zealand	v.	Italy	Marseille	13:45	...–...
9 September	Scotland	v.	Portugal	St Etienne	18:00	...–...
12 September	Italy	v.	Romania	Marseille	20:00	...–...
15 September	New Zealand	v.	Portugal	Lyon	13:00	...–...
18 September	Scotland	v.	Romania	Edinburgh	21:00	...–...
19 September	Italy	v.	Portugal	Paris	20:00	...–...
23 September	Scotland	v.	New Zealand	Edinburgh	17:00	...–...
25 September	Romania	v.	Portugal	Toulouse	20:00	...–...
29 September	New Zealand	v.	Romania	Toulouse	13:00	...–...
29 September	Scotland	v.	Italy	St Etienne	21:00	...–...

Final Group C table

	P	W	L	D	PF	PA	Pts
C1							
C2							
C3							
C4							
C5							

Fill-in Tournament Chart

GROUP D

Date	Match			Venue	Time	Result
7 September	France	v.	Argentina	St Denis	21:00	...–...
9 September	Ireland	v.	Namibia	Bordeaux	20:00	...–...
11 September	Argentina	v.	Georgia	Lyon	20:00	...–...
15 September	Ireland	v.	Georgia	Bordeaux	21:00	...–...
16 September	France	v.	Namibia	Toulouse	21:00	...–...
21 September	France	v.	Ireland	St Denis	21:00	...–...
22 September	Argentina	v.	Namibia	Marseille	21:00	...–...
26 September	Georgia	v.	Namibia	Lens	18:00	...–...
30 September	France	v.	Georgia	Marseille	15:00	...–...
30 September	Ireland	v.	Argentina	Paris	17:00	...–...

Final Group D table

	P	W	L	D	PF	PA	Pts
D1							
D2							
D3							
D4							
D5							

QUARTER-FINALS

Date					Venue	Time	Result
6 October	QF1	**B1**	v.	**A2**	Marseille	15:00	
			v.				...–...
6 October	QF2	**C1**	v.	**D2**	Cardiff	21:00	
			v.				...–...
7 October	QF3	**A1**	v.	**B2**	Marseille	15:00	
			v.				...–...
7 October	QF4	**D1**	v.	**C2**	St Denis	21:00	
			v.				...–...

SEMI-FINALS

Date					Venue	Time	Result
13 October	SF1	**W QF1**	v.	**W QF2**	St Denis	21:00	
			v.				...–...
14 October	SF2	**W QF3**	v.	**W QF4**	St Denis	21:00	
			v.				...–...

THIRD PLACE PLAY-OFF

Date					Venue	Time	Result
19 October	Bronze	**L SF1**	v.	**L SF2**	Paris	21:00	
			v.				...–...

WORLD CUP FINAL

Date					Venue	Time	Result
20 October	Final	**W SF1**	v.	**W SF2**	St Denis	21:00	
			v.				...–...

WORLD CHAMPIONS 2007

PICTURE CREDITS/ANSWERS

THE PUBLISHERS WOULD LIKE TO THANK THE FOLLOWING SOURCES FOR THEIR KIND PERMISSION TO REPRODUCE THE PICTURES IN THIS BOOK.

Action Images: 14b; /Eddie Keogh/Reuters: 15r; /Jason O'Brien: 34; /Jose Manuel Ribeiro/Reuters: 43; /Lee Smith: 15l

Alamy Images: /Michael Jenner: 61t

Corbis Images: /Gail Mooney: 60t; /Michel Setboun: 60b

Getty Images: /Odd Andersen/AFP: 16, 19; /Gabriel Bouys/AFP: 44; /Tom Brakefield: 77(16); /Jeff Brass: 29c; /Simon Bruty: 68tr; /Jon Buckle: 1; /Glenn Campbell/AFP: 27; /Russell Cheyne: 67; /Mike Clarke/AFP: 35; /Phil Cole: 30; /Mark Dadswell: 24; /Dorling Kindersley: 77(8); /Johannes Eisele/AFP: 4; /Alfred Eisenstaedt/Time & Life Pictures: 6; /Bob Elsdale/Photonica: 63t; /Darren England: 32; /Gallo Images: 23r; /Paul Gilham: 17t;

/Georges Gobet/AFP: 66; /Mike Hewitt: 33r; /Jeff Hunter/The Image Bank: 59; /Iconica: 63b; /Jimmy Jeong: 26; /Koichi Kamoshida: 40; /Paul Kane: 47r; /Ross Land: 36; /Warren Little: 38; /Alex Livesey: 51; /Chris McGrath: 50; /Damien Meyer/AFP: 37c, 45c, 55; /Paul Nicklen/National Geographic: 77(18); /Peter Parks: 25c; /Ryan Pierse: 29r; /David Rogers: 11, 12b, 23c, 25r, 28, 33c, 39c, 41r; /Norbert Rosing/National Geographic: 77(14); /David Silverman: 77(7); /Johannes Simon/AFP: 77(17); /Robin Smith/Stone: 77(11); /Stringer: 2-3; /Phil Walter: 77(4); /William West/AFP: 61b, 70, 77(3)

iStockphoto: 5, 10, 18, 52, 53, 58l, 58r, 62l, 62r, 64, 71, 77(9), 77(10), 77(12), 77(13), 79

Mary Evans Picture Library: /Bill Meadows: 9b

PA Photos: /Matthew Ashton: 14tl, 14r; /Mark Baker/AP: 37r; /Julien Behal: 74; /Angus Blackburn: 17b; /Delly Carr: 72; /Niall Carson: 77(1);

/Michael Cooper: 41c; /John Cowpland/AP: 77(6); /Steve Cuff: 65; /David Davies: 20, 21r, 31r, 49c, 69; /Adam Davy: 77(2); /Mike Egerton: 77(5), 80; /Christophe Ena/AP: 45r; /Nigel French: 42; /Alastair Grant/AP: 21c; /Themba Hadebe/AP: 22; /Tom Hevezi/AP: 48; /Tom Honan: 12t, 46; /Ross Kinnaird: 57r, 68l; /Kipa Press: 9t; /Tony Marshall: 31c, 73; /Toby Melville: 68b; /Gouhier Nicolas/Abaca: 49r; /Phil Noble: 8; /S&G/Alpha: 54, 56tl, 56br, 57tl; /Ross Setford/AP: 47c; /Neal Simpson: 57bl, 75; /John Walton: 76; /Steve Welsh: 39r

Photolibrary.com: /Chris McLennan: 77(15)

EVERY EFFORT HAS BEEN MADE TO ACKNOWLEDGE CORRECTLY AND CONTACT THE SOURCE AND/OR COPYRIGHT HOLDER OF EACH PICTURE AND CARLTON BOOKS LIMITED APOLOGISES FOR ANY UNINTENTIONAL ERRORS OR OMISSIONS WHICH WILL BE CORRECTED IN FUTURE EDITIONS OF THIS BOOK.

PICTURE QUIZ

1. Mystery Players (top row, l–r): Rafael Ibanez (France), John Hayes (Ireland), Mils Muliaina (New Zealand); bottom row (l–r): Stirling Mortlock (Australia), Jason Robinson (England), Percy Montgomery (S. Africa).

2. Say it with Flowers (l–r): England (Red Rose), Scotland (Thistle), Wales (Daffodil), Japan (Cherry Blossom), Ireland (Clover, four-leafed, of course), Namibia (Welwitschias – a flowering desert plant).

3. Spotter's Guide (top row, l–r): South Africa (Springboks), Argentina (Pumas, mountain lion), Tonga (Sea eagles); bottom row (l–r): Australia (Wallabies), Portugal (Wolves), United States (Eagles).

ANSWERS

1. David Kirk (New Zealand); 2. Grant Fox (New Zealand, 126); 3. Australia, 126; 4. Nick Farr-Jones; 5. Marc Ellis (New Zealand); 6. Gavin Hastings (Scotland, 227); 7. Jonah Lomu (New Zealand, 15); 8. Jannie de Beer (South Africa, 6 v. England in 1999); 9. Jason Leonard (England, 22); 10. Ralph Keyes (Ireland, 68 points); 11. Thierry Lacroix (France, 112); 12. Joel Stransky; 13. Rory Underwood (England) and David Campese (Australia); 14. Simon Culhane (New Zealand, 45); 15. Japan (16); 16. Gonzalo Quesada (Argentina, 102); 17. Stade de France, Paris, 75,000; 18. Michael Jones (New Zealand v. Italy); 19. Jonny Wilkinson (England), 113); 20. Lote Tuqiri (Australia) and Jason Robinson (England).